✔ KU-449-024

Birmingham Repertory Theatre Company
presents

Confidence

By Judy Upton

First Performance at
The Door, Birmingham Repertory Theatre
on 23 September 1998

SUPPORTED BY
THE NATIONAL LOTTERY
THROUGH
THE **ARTS COUNCIL**
OF ENGLAND

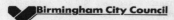
◆**Birmingham City Council**   WEST MIDLANDS ARTS

Providing Theatre for Birmingham

The Door

Confidence

by Judy Upton

Wed 23 Sep - Wed 25 Nov

'...So what do you want to be? The kicker or the kicked?'

Join the schemers and dreamers on the seafront, as another summer season begins and there's serious money to be made. Amongst the paint-peeling kiosks on the prom, Ella arrives like an erotic whirlwind, hellbent on securing the elusive jackpot. But everyone else is raising their game too and, as events race towards an explosive conclusion, a pet hamster lies frozen amongst the melting Mivvis.

Award-winning playwright Judy Upton's many prizes include the George Devine Award in 1993, two Guinness Awards and most recently the Open Stages Competition in 1997 which she won with her play *To Blusher With Love*.
Director: Anthony Clark
Designer: Patrick Connellan
Lighting: Tim Mitchell

After Dark: Tue 24 Nov (post show)

Twins

by Maureen Lawrence

Wed 7 Oct - Wed 18 Nov

'We're like a pantomime horse with two front ends. We don't fit the bill.'

Perched in the attic cluttered with their last few remaining heirlooms, Mimi and Gigi await the imminent arrival of the men who will repossess their home. But, Gigi believes, their hopelessly tangled lives, a husband tasted by them both and her last, mad spending spree mean that they are going to have to finally face facts. Elegant and sharply funny , Twins explores a relationship that runs through three very different solutions to the one problem.

Maureen Lawrence's previous work has been performed at both the Derby Playhouse and West Yorkshire Playhouse and her play *Resurrection* was the winner of the LWT Plays on Stage Award.
Director: Simon Usher
Designer: Lucy Weller
Lighting: Tim Mitchell

After Dark: Tue 17 Nov (post show)

Down Red Lane

by Kate Dean

Wed 28 Oct - Sat 28 Nov

*'We've made it. We've f**kin' made it. Two thousand f**kin' years n' we made it'*

It is Christmas 1999, not that you'll see any tinsel in the Red Lane Quarry - a time of reflection, fear and the odd splutter of hope. Through the dense winter fog, Spider and his ragbag of mates emerge, killing time with anything from a battered old saxophone to a bag of glue. Beneath them, the city pulses with distant light and movement - as it prepares for the celebration of the century.

Winner of a Special Prize in the Mobil Playwriting competition, *Down Red Lane* is just one of many award-winning plays by Kate Dean. Her play Rough (winner of the John Whiting Award) was produced in the Birmingham Rep Studio in 1994.
Director: Anthony Clark
Designer: Patrick Connellan
Lighting: Tim Mitchell

After Dark: Tue 10 Nov (post show

Sounds In Session

by Tyrone Huggins and The Theatre of Darkness

Thu 10 Dec - Sat 12 Dec

Theatre for the twenty-first century

Tanya's been on TOTP. Twice! She's also heard Black Voices. She wanted to do what Prince did. Turn her back on the whole bloody lot! She almost did what Jacko did. Turned her self white!
She has to prove at least one thing. She is in control.

Set in a grubby basement recording studio, three people gather to record one track that will change their lives. But which track? Written as a twelvetrack album Sounds...In Session pollutes your ear with what really controls the music biz...the technology !
Director: Tyrone Huggins
Design: Kendra Ullyart

Fourteen Songs, Two Weddings And A Funeral

Tamasha Theatre Company and Birmingham Repertory Theatre Company

Tue 15 Dec - Sat 9 Jan

The blockbuster Bollywood movie comes to the stage with a new English adaptation. Tear jerking melodrama, song, dance, comedy, tragedy, glamour, romance, lavish sets and sparkling costumes. Birmingham Rep and Tamasha Theatre Company have co-produced four new plays over the past five years - *Shaft of Sunlight*, *A Yearning*, *Tainted Dawn* and the multi- award winning *East is East* by Ayub Khan-Din.

Adapted from the film *Hum Aapke Hain Koun* for the stage by Sudha Bhuchar and Kristine Landon-Smith.
Director and Choreographer: Kristine Landon-Smith
Set Design: Sue Mayes
Lighting Design: Paul Taylor
Musical Director: Colin Sell

After Dark: Tue 5 Dec (post show)

De Profundis

Moving Theatre

13 - 29 Jan

Written in Reading Gaol to Wilde's lover and nemesis Alfred Douglas, *De Profundis* is both and astonishing tour-de-force of self-analysis and a passionate cry for us to re-examine all our attitudes and assumptions about crime and punishment.

Edited by Merlin Holland
Performed by Corin Redgrave
Music Composed by Jonathan Goldstein
Each performance will be followed by a discussion on the issues raised.

Just, Not Fair

Moving Theatre

11 - 30 Jan

Jim Robinson, one of the Bridgewater Four who won their freedom in 1997 after a marathon campaign proving their innocence, has fashioned *Just, Not Fair* with director Jessica Dromgoole and actor Malcolm Tierney.

It is an extraordinary monologue about his life including 18 years spent in prison and his time on the outside.
Production Design: Phillippe Brandt
Lighting Design: Jim Simmons
Each performance will be followed by a discussion on the issues raised in the play.

Confidence
By Judy Upton

CAST

Ruby Alison Lintott

Edwin Michael Mears

Ben Robin Pirongs

Ella Jody Watson

Dean Zoot Lynam

Director Anthony Clark

Designer Patrick Connellan

Lighting Design Tim Mitchell

Assistant Director Phil Tinline

Stage Manager Niki Ewen

Deputy Stage Manager Ruth Morgan

Assistant Stage Manager Daniel Precious

For my family

Judy Upton
Author

Judy's first stage play *Everlasting Rose*
was produced at London New Play
Festival in 1992. In 1994 she won the
George Devine Award for *Ashes And
Sand*, which was produced in that year at
the Royal Court Theatre Upstairs, and the
Verity Bargate award for *Bruises*, which
was co-produced by the Royal Court and
Soho Theatre Company at the Theatre
Upstairs in 1995. Judy's other stage plays
are: *Temple* - The Room, Richmond
Orange Tree, 1995; *The Shorewatchers
House* - The Red Room, Kentish Town,
1996; *Stealing Souls* - The Red Room,
1996; *Sunspots* - The Red Room, 1996
(transferred to Battersea Arts Centre);
People On The River - The Red Room at
the Finborough, 1997; *To Blusher With
Love* - (Winner of the 'Open Stages'
competition), Channel T.C at The Man In
The Moon, 1997; *Pig In The Middle* - Y
Touring, Schools tour and the House Of
Commons, 1998; *The Girlz* - The Room,
Richmond Orange Tree, 1998; *Know Your
Rights* - The Red Room at Battersea Arts
Centre, 1998.

Judy is currently writer in residence with
the Red Room. She has had two plays
broadcast on Radio 4 - *Tissue Memory*
and *Long Time Man*, and she is currently
under commission to adapt the novel *The
Serpentine Cave* by Jill Paton Walsh, as a
feature film for Double Scorpio
productions.

Alison Lintott
Ruby

Born: London

Trained: Central School Of Speech & Drama

For Birmingham Repertory Theatre: *Mary in Johnny Watkins Walks On Water*

Theatre: Rita in *Lonely Hearts* (Chesterfield); Mabel and Lady Chudleigh in *Plunder* (Savoy Theatre, London & National Tour); Lily in *Amongst Barbarians* (Workshop Production - The Drill Hall)

TV: *The Alchemist*; *Night Work*; *A Touch of Frost*; *Kavanagh QC*; *The Bill*

Film: *Underground*

Jody Watson
Ella

Trained: Central School of Speech and Drama

First professional engagement since graduating in 1998.

Prior to Training: Member of the Chickenshed Theatre Company; Chorus with the English National Opera at the London Coliseum.

Robin Pirongs
Ben

For Birmingham Repertory Theatre: Ron McNeil in *Divine Right*; Cecco in *Peter Pan*; Ape/Ivor in *Playing By The Rules*; Mick in *Big Maggie*; Sam in *Nervous Woman* and Deputy in *Grapes of Wrath*; Gambero in *Pinocchio*, Snowflake in *The Wizard of Oz*.

Theatre: Henry Pratt in *Second From Last In The Sack Race* (Harrogate); Teenage Scrooge in *A Christmas Carol*

(Octagon); Mark Anthony in *Grace* (Edinburgh/BAC/Arts West End); The Fool in *The Comic Mysteries* (Oxford St Co); Billy/Reg in *End Of The Pier* and Norman in *And a Nightingale Sang* (both at Cheltenham); Connie/Musician in *Grapes of Wrath*; Oliver in *I Have Been Here Before*; Malcolm in *Bedroom Farce*; Flute in *A Midsummer Night's Dream* (all for Northcott Theatre). Other roles include Gazza in *Wicked Year* (Royal National Theatre); Ernst Ludvig in *Cabaret* (Bolton)

TV: *The Bill*; *Hale and Pace*; *Real McCoy*; *Low Level Panic*; *2.4 Children*.

Michael Mears
Edwin

Trained: Drama Centre, London

First Appearance for Birmingham Repertory Theatre

Theatre: The Hungarian director in *Goodbye Girl* (Albery, West End). Also includes seasons at the RSC; West Yorkshire Playhouse; Nottingham Playhouse; Leicester Haymarket and the Victoria Stoke-on-Trent; a year with Actors Touring Company playing both Malvolio and Orsino in *Twelfth Night*; all over Britain and in the Far East. Christ in the 1984 Mystery Plays Cycle, Fagin in *Oliver!* Sherlock Holmes in *Hound of The Baskervilles* (Coventry Belgrade). Sir Amorous La Foole in Ben Jonson's *Silent Woman* (RSC, Swan); Minister of the Interior in *Clockwork Orange* (RSC Barbican); Charlie in *Conversations With My Father* (Scarborough and the Old Vic). His two solo plays *Tomorrow We Do The Sky* and *Soup* were award-winning hits at the Edinburgh Festival and in London, before being broadcast on Radio 4.

Film: *Four Weddings and a Funeral*; *Little Dorrit*; *The Old Curiosity Shop* and *Queen*

Of Hearts; Kidnapped

TV: *The Lenny Henry Show; Sharpe; Inspector Morse; Chelmsford 123.*

Radio; His new solo play *A Slight Tilt To The Left* is to be broadcast on Radio 4 early next year.

Zoot Lynam
Dean

Trained: The Anna Scher Theatre

For Birmingham Repertory Theatre: *The Winslow Boy* (transferred to West Yorkshire Playhouse)

Theatre: *The Warp* (dir. Ken Campbell); *Makbed* (dir. Ken Campbell); *Fairytale Heart* (Hampstead Theatre)

Film: *Being Human; The Secret Garden; Scheer*

TV: *Thirty Years to Life; The Bill; Midsomer Murders; Soldier Soldier; Casualty; Willows in Winter; Jackanory; You Me and Him; MUD; The Biz*

Radio: *Something Understood* (Radio 4)

Anthony Clark
Director

Since joining Birmingham Repertory Theatre Company in 1990 as an Associate Director, Anthony has directed *The Seagull, Of Mice and Men, Macbeth, Saturday Sunday Monday, Cider With Rosie* (national tour), *The Threepenny Opera, The Pied Piper, My Mother Said I Never Should, The Grapes of Wrath, The Atheist's Tragedy,* (1994 TMA/Martini Award for Best Director), *The Playboy of the Western World, Peter Pan, Pygmalion, The Red Balloon* (1995 TMA /Martini Award for Best Show for Children and Young People), *The Entertainer,*

Gentlemen Prefer Blondes, Pinocchio, Julius Caesar and new plays: *True Brit, Rough, Playing By the Rules* (Mentorn First Night Production Award), *Nervous Women* and *Syme* (a co-production with the Royal National Theatre Studio).

Anthony graduated from Manchester University Drama Department (RSC Buzz Goodbody Award '79), spent two years directing at the Orange Tree Theatre, London and a year working with Tara Arts before being appointed Artistic Director of Contact Theatre in Manchester in 1984. At Contact Theatre his wide range of productions included new plays: *Face Value, Two Wheel Tricycle, McAlpine's Fusiliers, Green and Homeland,* classics: *Mother Courage and Her Children, Blood Wedding, A Midsummer Night's Dream, The Duchess of Malfi, To Kill a Mockingbird* (European premiere - Manchester Evening News Best Production Award 87) and *Oedipus Rex.* His freelance directing credits include: *Dr Faustus* (Young Vic), *To Kill A Mockingbird* (Greenwich Theatre), *The Snowman* (Leicester Haymarket), *The Red Balloon* (Bristol Old Vic), *The Day After Tomorrow, Mother Courage and her Children* and *The Red Balloon* for the Royal National Theatre, and *The Wood Demon* (West End).

As a writer he has had the following plays produced: *Hand it to Them, Wake* and a translation of Tolstoy's *The Power of Darkness* at the Orange Tree Theatre, *Tidemark* at the RSC Thoughtcrimes Festival, *A Matter of Life and Death* at the Royal National Theatre, *Green* and musical adaptations of *The Snowman, The Little Prince* and *The Red Balloon* at Contact Theatre in Manchester and *The Pied Piper* and *Pinocchio* at Birmingham Repertory Theatre.

Patrick Connellan
Designer

For Birmingham Repertory Theatre:
Rough; *Pygmalion*; *The Atheist's Tragedy*;
Cider With Rosie; *The Pied Piper*; *The
Grapes of Wrath*; *Nervous Women* and
Julius Caesar

Patrick won the Linbury Prize for stage
design in 1987 and has since worked
extensively in the West End and regional
theatre. In 1989 Patrick designed the
indoor production of *Der Fliegende
Hollander* for Bregenzer Festspiele. His
most recent theatre credits include: *Silas
Marner*; *She Stoops To Conquer*; *Leader
of the Pack*; *Neville's Island* and *The
Wedding* (Belgrade Theatre Coventry);
Misery; *A Passionate Woman* (Comedy
Theatre); *Salad Days* (Vaudeville
Theatre); *Conduct Unbecoming*; (National
Tour); *Coriolanus*; *When We Are Married*
and *The Rivals* (West Yorkshire
Playhouse); *Misery* (Haymarket Theatre
Leicester); *Macbeth*; *Twelfth Night* and *I
Have Been Here Before* (Mercury Theatre
Colchester); *Time and the Conways*
(Octagon Bolton). Future productions
include *Limestone Cowboy* at The
Belgrade Theatre Coventry and *Top Girls*
at Salisbury Playhouse and The Drum
Plymouth.

Tim Mitchell
Lighting Designer

Tim is currently lighting designer in
residence at Birmingham Repertory
Theatre where he has lit many
productions, these include:

Frozen, *Whisper of Angels Wings*, *The
Cherry Orchard*, *True Brit*, *Dr Jekyll and
Mr Hyde*, *Romeo and Juliet*, *The
Merchant of Venice*, *Macbeth*, *Old Times*,
Peter Pan and *The Atheist's Tragedy*

(Gold Medal Winner at the 1995 Prague
Quadrennial)

Other productions include: *Romeo and
Juliet* (RSC), *The Red Balloon* and *The
Alchemist* (Royal National Theatre),
Outside of Heaven, *Inventing a New
Colour* and *Young Writers Festival* (Royal
Court Theatre), *Someone to Watch Over
Me*, *When We are Married*, *Landslide*,
The Winslow Boy and *The Entertainer*
(West Yorkshire Playhouse) *Dead Funny*,
Wallflowering and *Tess of the
D'Urbervilles* (Salisbury Playhouse), *Song
at Sunset* and the *New Directions Season*
(Hampstead Theatre), Adam Bede, *A
Passionate Woman*, *The Importance of
Being Earnest*, *Les Liaisons Dangereuses*
and *Our Boys* (Derby Playhouse), *A
Soldiers Song* (Theatre Royal Stratford
East), *WodeHouse on Broadway* (BBC
TV/Theatre Royal Plymouth), *As You Like
It* and *Anthony and Cleopatra* (English
Shakespeare Company).

Phil Tinline
Assistant Director

As Assistant Director at the Orange Tree
Theatre, Richmond: *What the Heart
Feels*; *Family Circles*; *She'll be Coming
Round The Mountain*; *Romeo & Juliet*;
The Outside; *A Midsummer Night's
Dream*

Other directing credits include: *A Glass of
Water*; *She'll Be Wearing Silk Pyjamas*
(Orange Tree); *Shakespeare for
Breakfast* (Edinburgh Fringe), *Lavender
Song* (Prince Theatre); *Rum and Vodka*,
Newsrevue (Canal Cafe Theatre)

Phil is at Birmingham Rep for a year
under the Regional Theatre Young
Director Scheme, before which he ran the
Canal Cafe Theatre in West London.

The Birmingham RepertoryTheatre Company
Introducing

The Door

Since it was founded in 1913 Birmingham Repertory Theatre Company has been a leading national company. Its programming has introduced a range of new and foreign plays to the British theatre repertoire, and it has been a springboard for many internationally famous actors, designers and directors.

As the arts in Birmingham have grown in stature, with the opening of Symphony Hall, the achievements of the City of Birmingham Symphony Orchestra and the arrival of the Birmingham Royal Ballet so there has been massive investment in the resident theatre company.

Now the company can present classic, new and discovery plays on a scale appropriate to one of the largest acting spaces in Europe , as well as a consistent programme of new theatre in its studio, by some of the brightest contemporary talent To celebrate this, the space has a new name and a new look.

The Door's programme seeks to find a young and culturally diverse audience for the theatre, through the production of new work in an intimate, flexible space - work, that reflects, defines and enhances their experience of the world while introducing them to the possibilities of the medium.

New Work at Birmingham Repertory Theatre
- past, present and future

In recent years, this theatre has produced a range of popular, award-winning and critically acclaimed new plays. These include *Divine Right* (1996), Peter Whelan's examination of the future of the British monarchy, Kate Dean's *Rough* (1994), Bryony Lavery's *Nothing Compares To You* (1995), Debbie Isitt's *Squealing Like A Pig* (1996), Ayub Khan-Din's *East is East* (1996) (co-production with Tamasha Theatre Company and the Royal Court Theatre, London), Ken Blakeson's *True Brit* (1997) and Nick Stafford's *The Whisper of Angel's Wings* (1997).

This year, our production of *Frozen* by Bryony Lavery which starred Anita Dobson, Tom Georgeson and Josie Lawrence was unaminously praised for its bravery, humanity and humour in exploring the intertwined experiences of a mother, the murderer of her daughter and the psychiatrist who treats him.

From this autumn the increased level of financial support for the theatre means that we can plan a range of creative projects and initiatives across the full range of theatre's spaces and activities, supporting both the artists who create new work and the audiences for it.

One example is **Transmissions** - a pilot project in which young people in Birmingham aged from 7 to 25 will write their own plays alongside experienced professional playwrights with the chance to see their work performed here at the theatre. Another is the theatre's attachment scheme for writers. This enables both younger and more experienced playwrights to explore new ideas and directions with our support and with the ultimate aim of transforming them into plays for our stages.

If you would like more information on this of other aspects of our work, please contact us on 0121 236 6771 x2108/2109

Ben Payne
Literary Manager

Frozen: Anita Dobson and Tom Georgeson
Photo: Robert Day

The Whisper of Angels' Wings: Tricia Kelly and Michael Cashman
Photo: Robert Day

The Birmingham Repertory Theatre gratefully acknowledges the support of the Sir Barry Jackson Trust in its new work development programme

Supported by
THE
SIR BARRY JACKSON
TRUST

Birmingham Rep Young Writers Group

This autumn sees the relaunch of The Rep's Young Writers' Group. Building on its past successes the group will also be integrating the writers' work more closely with other new writing and production activities in The Door.

The young writers' group has an illustrious past. During 1996 - 98 the creative writing tutor was local writer Sarah Woods, whose plays *Grace, Nervous Women* and *Bidding and Binding* were performed at the Rep. For the past two years the Rep has also run a young writers' festival called Hot Off The Page. Highlights of the work produced during the festival include *Redemption Denied* by Lucy Hughes, which took a hard hitting view of Birmingham drug culture, while *No Time to Say Goodbye* by Rachael Owen told the story of a young evacuee who rebels against his mother's religious fanaticism. Marie Clarke's *Apocalypse* took a satirical view of 90s female obsessions, careers, figures, boyfriends and food. In 1998 the youth theatre also performed Louise Ramsden's play *The Highwayman* - a black comedy about a disabled spinster who dreams of escape from the sister she is bound to care for and the hidden secret that still overshadows their lives. Louise has workshopped other pieces with professional actors and in '96 her play *My Baby Mine* received a reading at the Royal Court Theatre Upstairs.

Many members of the Young Writers' Group have continued to develop their writing through higher education courses such as Theatre Arts or Drama at University.

Now the theatre is in a position to widen access to the group and to restructure the group's activities for regular tutorials by a resident tutor with visiting or guest tutors from the profession, in addition to specialised skills development workshops with other theatre practitioners such as directors and actors.

For more information about the Birmingham Rep Young Writers Group please call Liz Ingrams at The Rep on 0121 236 6771 x2109.

Transmissions

A festival of playwriting by young people

September to November 1998

As Birmingham's only venue dedicated to new writing The Door is investing in writers of the future, with an exclusive festival of playwriting for young people.

Something for all ages

Plays will be workshopped and developed with five primary schools, a Saturday playwriting project run for youth drama group members (drawn from Stage 2, Yeh-leh-leh Theatre Company, Kaos Theatre Company, SAMPAD, Swanshurst School and Streetwise Theatre Company), and a relaunched young writers group.

A chance to work alongside professionals

Everyone involved will work in collaboration with the Birmingham Rep's literature and education departments as well as their designated tutors. These professionals have been chosen for their ability to write, direct and work well with young people and include some of the region's most talented artists. Those taking part include local playwright and performer Lorna Laidlaw, Peter Wynne-Wilson, Maya Chowdhry (author of Birmingham Rep's most recent community production *Kaahini*), Glen Supple (a Royal Court Young People's Theatre director), Noel Grieg, Theresa Heskins and Sarah Woods.

Developing and performing new work

The project will have a different emphasis depending on the age range of the people involved. Children's groups will develop plays in conjunction with their teachers and tutors, other groups will develop and rehearse a series of linked scenes. Meanwhile young playwrights will work on a fifteen minute script and receive one to one tuition from playwright Sarah Woods with additional skills development workshops with other writers and practitioners. The best pieces will be directed by Theresa Heskins and rehearsed at the end of November, and others will receive rehearsed readings directed by an 'in-house' director over the two week period. The festival will culminate with performances at The Rep involving both professional and young actors.

For more information about this and any other Education activities please call Rachel Gartside, Head of Education on 0121 236 6771.

From Stage to Page

A stimulating programme of work for further and higher education groups to accompany the three new plays premiering in rep in The Door: CONFIDENCE by Judy Upton, TWINS, by Maureen Lawrence, and DOWN RED LANE, by Kate Dean.

What's On Offer?

Workshops

If you make block bookings, two workshops will be offered. The first involves an exploration of the content of the text, themes and structure etc. to be led by the Rep's Education Department and held at your college. The second will be run by a writer and the Rep's Associate Director Anthony Clark and will explore ideas behind the writing and the process of producing the piece from page to stage. These second workshops will take place at the theatre.

Scripts

Scripts will be produced for each play, and will provide an opportunity for further study of the text's form and content.

Discounted Tickets

Tickets are available at just £5.00 per performance. With tickets normally at £9/£7 this represents a substantial discount.

Unbeatable Value

Tickets, workshops and scripts are included in the price of the package. From Stage to Page is a pro-active approach to serve mutual needs – an opportunity to tackle your curriculum in a unique, accessible way, at the cutting edge of contemporary theatrical culture – all for just £25.00 per student (minimum 15 students).

After Darks

Held after the show with the company. Ask anything you've ever wanted to know about the play...an immediate, informal and inviting opportunity to question the play and the players - and it's free! After Darks in The Door will usually involve an expert panel who can debate the issues or concerns of the piece and set it in a wider context. Check the brochure or call our Box Office on 0121 236 4455 for dates.

Birmingham Repertory Theatre

DIRECTORS OF BIRMINGHAM REPERTORY THEATRE LIMITED
David Waine (Chair)
Cllr Brenda Clarke
Norman Hawkins
Tyrone Huggins
John A James
Prof Joel Kaplan
Michael Lowe
Dr Vayu Naidu-Banfield
Cllr Alan Rudge
Bob Southgate
Vanessa Whitburn
Toyah Wilcox

TRUSTEES OF SIR BARRY JACKSON TRUST
Roger Burman CBE (Chair)
Cllr J.E.C. Alden (Hon Secretary)
Ian King (Hon Treasurer)
L A Chorley
David Edgar
Kate Horton
Dr R B Leach
Mr P Baird
David Waine
Graham Winteringham

TRUSTEES OF BIRMINGHAM REPERTORY THEATRE FOUNDATION
Sue Battle OBE
Berard Carey
Graham Green
John Gunn(Chair)
David Haggett
Richard Ireland
John A James
David Rouse
Sandra Squires
David Waine

ARTISTIC DIRECTOR
Bill Alexander

EXECUTIVE PRODUCER
John Stalker

ASSOCIATE ARTISTIC DIRECTOR
Anthony Clark

LITERARY MANAGER
Ben Payne

LITERARY ASSISTANT
Liz Ingrams

RESIDENT DRAMATIST
Nick Stafford +

RYTDS TRAINEE DIRECTOR
Philip Tinline *

PROJECT MANAGER
Ros Robins

ASSOCIATE PRODUCER
Wiff Maton

SECRETARIAL ASSISTANTS
Audrey Howkins
Sue Johnson

HEAD OF FINANCE & ADMINISTRATION
Peter Winckles

FINANCE MANAGER (TECHNICAL ASSISTANCE)
Stuart Clarke

FINANCE OFFICER
Ruth Wood

FINANCE ASSISTANT
Diane Baker

HEAD OF EDUCATION
Rachel Gartside

ACTING EDUCATION OFFICER
Annie Emery

HEAD OF MARKETING AND DEVELOPMENT
Amie Smart

BUSINESS DEVELPOMENT AND SPONSORSHIP MANAGER
Joanne Aubrey

DEVELOPMENT ADMINISTRATOR
Karen Stafford

MARKETING OFFICER
Vanessa Walters

PRESS & MEDIA OFFICER
Jane Spence
0121 237 1525

MARKETING ASSISTANT
Jane Macpherson

SALES MANAGER
Rachel Foster

DEPUTY SALES MANAGER
Eddie Lee

SALES TEAM
Abigail Craven
Kim Grogan
Caroline Jester
Eileen Minnock
Andrea Pitt
Lucy Pointon

THEATRE MANAGER
Gary Stewart

HOUSE MANAGER
Gill Bourbage

DEPUTY HOUSE MANAGER
Nigel Cairns

SENIOR FRONT OF HOUSE ATTENDANT
Val Munday

FRONT OF HOUSE ATTENDANTS
Denise Belford
Brenda Bradley
Mary Gordon
Marlene Gregory
Thanks also to our team of Front of House casual attendants and firemen

ACTING HEAD OF MAINENANCE
Colin Williamson

MAINTENANCE ASSISTANT
Colin Williamson

STAGE DOOR
Robert Flynn
Albert Hearn
Fraser Paterson

PRODUCTION MANAGER
John Pitt

STAGE MANAGER
Sally Isern
Niki Ewen

DEPUTY STAGE MANAGER
Louise Bann
Ruth Morgan

ASSISTANT STAGE MANAGER
Emma Routledge
Daniel Precious

STAGE SUPERVISOR
Michael Allison

STAGE TECHNICIANS
Ian Barron
John Forster
Kevin Smith

TRANSPORT
Pete Triance

RESIDENT LIGHTING DESIGNER
Tim Mitchell

ELECTRICS SUPERVISOR
Miike Fowler

SOUND ENGINEER
Dave Tinson

LIGHTING TECHICIANS
Steve Allsop
Matthew Mawdsley
Phillip Swoffer

HEAD OF CONSTRUCTION AND DESIGN
Charles MacCall

HEAD OF WORKSHOP/STOCK CONTROLLER
Craig Blackledge

DEPUTY HEAD OF WORKSHOP
Paul Huckerby

CARPENTERS/METALWORKERS
Madelaine Loving
Lewis Pierpoint
Emma Warson

HEAD SCENIC ARTIST
David Williams

DEPUTY HEAD SCENIC ARTIST
Christopher Tait

HEAD OF PROPS
Stuart Waggett

DEPUTY & ARMOURER
Alan Bennett

PROP MAKER
Helen Jones

HEAD OF WARDROBE
Sue Nightingale

DEPUTY HEAD OF WARDROBE
Karen Stevenett

WARDROBE ASSISTANTS
Julie Dean
Margaret Gillham
Cat Morgan

WIGS AND MAKEUP
Andrew Whiteoak

CATERING
0121 644 6464
(Olivier's Restaraunt, Rep Cafe, Theatre Bars & Hospitality)

MANAGER
John Lander

DEPUTY CATERING MANAGER
Sam Bates

HEAD CHEF
Aiden Callaghan

DUTY MANAGERS
Elizabeth Criddle
Margaret Harmitt
Marie Bailey

GREEN ROOM
Pete Davies

CLEANING
We Are Cleaning (GB) Ltd

Acting Company Richard Armitage, Rakie Ayola, Glenn Chapman, Richard Da Costa, Martin Hutson, Andy Hockley, Jack Klaff, Alison Lintott, Zoot Lynam, John McAndrew, Richard McCabe, Michael Mears, Gerard Murphy, Anna Nicholas, Steven O'Neill, Robin Pirongs, John Quentin, Oliver Ryan, Adam Smethurst, Jody Watson. **Associate Artists** Michael Cashman, Jeffery Kissoon, Gerard Murphy, David Schofield
+Funded by the Arts Council of England *This theatre has the support of CENTRAL under the Regional Theatre Young Director Scheme administered by Channel Four Television.

Scene One

Left side of the stage is an ice-cream kiosk. **Ella**, *eighteen, and* **Dean**, *sixteen, are inside it. Right is a café – with an aquarium and fruit machine. Outside the café are plastic tables with chairs and sun umbrellas stacked against them.*

Dean   So is it true then? (*Pause.*) About you being in the paper last year . . . in *colour* and everything. (*Pause.*) I mean, tits and *everything*?

Ella (*bleakly*)   Want a copy to wank over?

Dean   Yeah! . . . er if that's OK, I mean . . .

Ella   It was a rip off, right? I'm not even showing my nipples. Don't think the photographer believed me about my age and that. Just got my top pulled down a bit . . .

She demonstrates.

. . . and I'm kinda looking at the camera all pouty. I had to say 'big dog's cock' . . .

Dean *laughs.*

Ella   – Supposed to make you look like you're having dirty thoughts or something. I was thinking of the money.

Dean   That why you did it?

Ella   What other reason is there?

Dean   Well, that Shane bloke . . .

Ella   He's a nerd, but he has some good ideas.

Dean   It was his idea?

Ella   No, it was mine. See, Shane reads those geeky kind of mags, 'bout unexplained mysteries. You know – the sort which always have Gillian Anderson on the cover? Well, he'd read this stuff about a woman where everything she touched caught fire . . .

Dean   Spontaneous combustion? (*Hastily*.) Not that I read those magazines . . .

Ella   It wasn't *her* catching fire, just things around her. He was talking about it one night – saying that he reckoned we could fake something like that, and sell the story. So I got him to blow-torch an old bedsheet, and then take a polaroid of me in my undies, holding it up and looking pouty. Shane then writes to the paper . . . like 'Every time I have *wild*, *passionate* sex with my girl, she sets my bed on fire, *for real*.' They bought it . . . but not for as much as I thought they'd pay. Then my dad sees it and goes fucking spare . . . like grounds me for ever. Nasty old sod – I expect it turned him on or something.

Dean   But Shane, I mean, he's not . . . like your boyfriend or something?

Ella   God, no. Urh. I mean, he's great if you've got anything that's broke and needs fixing, but I couldn't shag a bloke who's into *Star Trek*.

Dean   Yeah, me neither . . . a bird, I mean . . . who was into all that stuff. (*A beat*.) So when're you going then?

Ella   Saturday morning.

Dean   Saturday! You can't go Saturday. There's Sophie's party, Saturday.

Ella   Yeah, well, this is an unmissable opportunity, Dean – Two free flights to the USA.

Dean   And you're taking that Stefan bloke – the pervy prison chef?

Ella   *Former* prison chef. Got himself sacked, hasn't he, stupid bastard. But the thing is, he's got this uncle with a firm that does the catering for film companies. In Hollywood.

Dean   . . . So you're gonna get into the movies – cool.

Ella   No, I'm gonna do some business.

Dean   Business?

Ella   It's the land of opportunity . . . I mean you can make a million out there . . . from selling garbage.

Dean   Yeah?

Ella   You just go round at night and empty film stars' dustbins. There's loads of collectors who'll pay a fortune for celebrity rubbish. I've got it all planned out. All I've got to do is ring up about our tickets, and we'll be on our way. Dad and Sandra'll get back from Ibiza on Monday and I'll be like long gone.

Dean   Look, Ella . . . I mean, I know your dad's a bastard and that . . . but didn't you still oughta at least leave him a note, or something . . .

Ella   Yeah, that's a thought . . . lay a false trail . . . I suppose I could leave him one saying I've decided to go away to college after all. Well, there's sure to be management courses in LA – I might do one, when I've made some money.

Dean   I'm gonna do a course.

Ella   When?

Dean *ducks down out of sight.*

Dean   I'm out of Calippos. Orange *and* lemon.

Ella   There's nobody about anyway. Why don't you close up, and we can sit on the beach?

Dean   No way. Beach is covered in tar, innit? I've still got it all over me black jeans.

Ella   Doesn't show though on black jeans, does it?

Dean   It's still sticky. Fluff and that sticks to it.

Ella   Urh.

Dean *ducks down out of sight again.*

Dean   The mint Cornettos look a bit soft.

Ella   Maybe those girls'll turn up.

Dean (*out of sight*)   No.

Ella   The short one wanted you.

Dean   No.

He stands up beside her again.

Which one was the short one?

Ella   Dark hair . . . blonde roots. Peeling a bit on her shoulders.

Dean   No.

Ella   Blue lace top . . .

Dean   Tits. Yeah. Her, yeah. (*Pause.*) No. I mean nice body, but no. God, her laugh.

Ella   Shit, yeah. She was *loud*.

Dean   Embarrassing. Without the laugh she'd be alright. But Jesus! Horrible, urg.

Ella   Are there any Flakes?

Dean (*out of sight*)   Don't start me on that again.

Ella   Are there?

Dean   You're asking for it.

Ella   So.

Ella *undoes the belt on her jeans. We can't see below her chest, because the serving hatch is in the way.*

Dean   Ow. You nearly had my eye out with your buckle.

Ella   Good.

She jiggles about.

Worst thing about new jeans, you can't undo the buttons without breaking your fucking nails. (*Pause.*) Dean!

Pause. She checks they're not being watched.

That's nice. Just stroke me.

Dean (*out of sight*)   Will you be coming back? I mean, you're not thinking of going for ever like?

Ella   Slower.

Dean   (*out of sight*)   I don't like slow.

Ella   Guys are different. Ahhh! What's that?

Dean   Cadbury's Flake.

Ella   Dean! Just stroke me. Don't stick it up. I mean, it'll break off or something. I don't want bits of chocolate dropping out me fanny all day.

Dean   Could put it in the freezer, make it hard, then it won't crumble.

Ella   Punter. Shit!

Ella *pulls up her jeans,* **Dean** *stands up, holding the Flake.*

Enter **Ben**.

Ben   Hi, our kid. How's tricks?

Dean *looks at* **Ella**.

Dean   Er, this is Ella. Ella – me brother Ben.

Ben   Ella . . . nice to meet you. You're helping Dean out in there?

Ella   Just offering him the benefit of my retail experience.

Ben   Yeah? Well, he's a bone-idle bastard, don't let him get you doing all his work for nothing. Now if it's a job you're looking for, I'm the man to ask. I'm sure I could find you something . . . In fact come to think of it, we could do with an extra hand in the café . . .

Dean   Helping Rubes?

Ella   Serving teas and washing up? Not really my thing.

Dean   Ella doesn't need a job. She's leaving at the weekend.

Ben   So you're just here on holiday, are you?

Ella   No, I live here.

Ben   You're a local girl then. Right.

Ella   So what about you . . . Ben. How come I've not seen you around?

Ben   You've just not been looking.

Dean *gives* **Ella** *the flake. He leaves the kiosk.*

Ben   But you're planning on leaving us then?

Dean *starts taking the café chairs off the tables, putting up the sun umbrellas.* **Ben** *stays at the hatch talking to* **Ella**.

Ella   On Saturday, yeah.

Ben   You'll miss my sister's party.

Ella   Sophie, yeah. Met her once or twice . . . but I wouldn't know anyone else there . . .

Dean   You'd know us.

Ella   . . . And 'cos I've met Dean . . . and you know he's a mate like, I'd have to get her a present . . . And it's not that I'm a tight wad . . . I just always find that stuff really hard . . . I never know what to get people. I know her like, but I don't really *know her*. What she likes and that.

Dean   You could just bring some beers.

Ella   But she's *almost* a friend, so that'd look a bit stingy.

Ben   Bring lots of beers. Bring some trips.

Ella   But they're for everyone. She should have something special. It's her birthday. Anyway, I probably won't be here.

Ben Yeah – shame that.

Ella Yeah?

Ben Yeah. (*Indicating the Cadbury's flake.*) Who's that for?

Ella Nobody.

Ben *takes the flake, bites off a bit.* **Ella** *is agog.*

Ella Ahhh!

Ben I haven't got her anything for her birthday yet, either.

Ella Hard, innit?

Ben I don't really know what girls of seventeen are into . . . apart from the obvious. She's just got so many CDs and things . . . I always end up getting one she's got. What did you get for your birthday?

Ella Me? I can't remember . . . Dean, what did I get for my birthday?

Dean Fuck knows.

Ella *looks down at her hand.*

Ella Shit. Right in front of me. This ring.

Ella *lets* **Ben** *see her ring.*

Ben That's nice. Expensive?

Ella Seventy quid.

Ben Shit.

Ella From my dad . . . He's always trying to outdo my mum, buying me expensive things. Trouble is, it was supposed to be my birthstone, but he fucked up big-time . . . got June's stone instead – fucking topaz, when mine's aquamarine.

Ben So topaz is Sophie's birthstone? Right . . .

Ben *looks at* **Ella**'s *hand.*

Ella   And I have all my jewellery set with aquamarines. Just my dad didn't know that, did he? Saw a nice ring in town in a second-hand place – like this but the right stone. Thirty quid.

Ben   That's reasonable.

Ella   Yeah, thirty quid's fine if you've *got* thirty quid. Maybe I'll take this one in and sell it. Trouble is they'll probably only give me fifteen for it. Those places are a fucking rip-off.

Ben   You're gonna sell that ring?

Ella   I don't know . . . I mean, fifteen for a seventy quid ring . . .

Ben   . . . yeah, look . . . wait a minute . . . Give me a proper look, up close like. Yeah, I reckon that could make a nice little present for Sophie . . . Dean, would Sophie like this ring? It's her birthstone.

Dean *looks at the ring.*

Dean   It's a nice ring.

Ella   Look, I can't let Sophie have it. I mean, if I was getting her a present . . . because I don't know her that well . . . I'd have give her something less expensive. Otherwise, she'd feel she had to get *me* something that costs a lot for my birthday, and it all gets stupid . . .

Ben   No, I meant I could give Sophie the ring. I've thirty quid . . .

Ben *delves in his pocket.*

Ella   Look, I can't take that sort of money off you.

Dean   It's alright, Ella. Ben's rich.

Ben   I wish.

Dean   You are. Against us you are.

Ella   Look, just give me twenty-five.

Ella *pulls at her ring.*

Ben   Are you sure?

Ella   Just help me get it off.

Ben *pulls the ring off* **Ella**'s *finger. She takes it from him, takes his hand, slides it on his little finger.* **Ben** *gives her the money.*

Blackout.

Scene Two

Evening. The café.

Ruby *(plump, twenty-one) is wiping down the café tables.*

Enter **Edwin**, *(forty-five), pale, thin, taking painful steps on crutches.*

Ruby *(without looking up)*   Sorry, we're closing.

Edwin *walks towards the fish tank. She follows.*

Ruby   Excuse me, I said . . .

Edwin *turns. She is shocked, recognising him.*

Ruby   Mr Bayliss! . . . Oh, I'm sorry.

Edwin   How are you, Ruby?

Ruby   Oh, I'm fine . . . how are you?

Edwin   Glad to be back.

Ruby   Yes. Er yes, I expect you are . . .

Awkward pause. **Edwin** *watches the fish.* **Ruby** *wipes the tables.*

. . . the ghost koi died . . . about a month ago. I've been cleaning them out every time it goes green and I got a better aerator like you said. They do seem to be swimming much faster since they've had that . . .

Edwin *is engrossed in the fish.*

Edwin   They've grown so much. Bronzino's enormous.
And Bellini.

Ruby   I hope I haven't overfed 'em. (*Pause.*) Would you
like a cup of tea, Mr Bayliss?

Edwin   No thanks, Ruby.

Ruby   A sandwich or anything? This morning's have
probably gone a bit dry, but I can make you some fresh
ones . . .

Edwin   No, it's alright.

Pause. **Ruby** *hovers.*

So . . . how've things been? Have you been busy?

Ruby   Oh yes . . . whenever the weather's nice I'm rushed
off my feet . . . 'specially since Ben sacked Naomi.

Edwin *runs his finger along the table top.*

Ruby   I have been dusting, and cleaning down all the
work surfaces every night. The health inspector came last
month and couldn't find a single thing to complain about.

Edwin   I'm very glad to hear it. Nevertheless it does badly
need a lick of paint around here. I can't believe how
battered and rundown everywhere looks . . . And I see we've
three kiosks, and two stall plots empty. I'll have to have
words with young Benjamin.

Ruby   You know Madame Zara's thinking of giving up
her booth at the end of the season?

Edwin   My God, is she really? . . . It won't be the same
without her. She was one of my dad's first tennants. Every
year May first to September thirtieth – never a day more or
a day less.

Ruby   She's amazing – her predictions. Told me I'd have
to say goodbye to someone close to me – then Hamish died
. . . You know, I used to be quite scared of her. I mean,
those piercing eyes . . .

Edwin   When I was a kid . . . actually I had a bit of a crush on Madame Zara . . .

Ruby *looks at him.*

Edwin   . . . And I've heard tales about her and my dad . . . but they might just be tales. I wonder why she's decided to call it a day.

Ruby   Two wettish summers in a row, she says.

Edwin   Maybe that's why the Randalls have gone . . . and those craft jewellery people.

Ruby   . . . unless it was rent increases.

Edwin (*sharply*)   What? I haven't put anyone's rent up in two years.

Ruby *is about to say something, but thinks better of it.*

Edwin   The place really seems to have changed, since I . . . since the summer before last. The people are different somehow . . .

Ruby   There's new families running the shooting gallery and the prize-every-time.

Edwin   I mean, the public have changed. I was up on the pier just now . . . it seems to be as packed as ever, but the atmosphere's different. There's no laughter, no smiles. Just anger . . .

Ruby   Well, this time of night they're all p . . . drunk as . . . as . . . aren't they?

Edwin   When I couldn't get out of some yob's way quick enough for his liking, I thought he was going to knock me down. . . . Well, perhaps it's just the hot weather making people short-tempered. Or perhaps I'm imagining it. (*Pause.*) Do you know if Ben's tried to get a new Punch and Judy man?

Ruby   I think he advertised at the start of the season. I still can't believe Harry drowned himself. He always had a smile on his face, didn't he?

Edwin *opens the fishfood pot.*

Ruby   Do you think maybe he was lonely?

Edwin *feeds the fish.* **Ruby** *moves to join him, but doesn't.*

Ruby   I'm . . . I'm glad you're back, Mr Bayliss.

He looks at her. She goes back to wiping a table. He watches the fish.

Blackout.

Scene Three

The same location as the two previous scenes.

Ella *and* **Dean** *are lying on the beach-front. The hatch on the ice-cream kiosk is closed, with a sign 'We're Shut – tough!' Blu-tacked across it.* **Ella** *is reading a book.* **Dean** *smears sunblock on her shoulders.*

Ella   Three bar, two bar, one bar.

Dean   My brother's a tosser, isn't he?

Ella   Nudge it, or drop it in, holding two reels. What? Ben? How old's he?

Dean   Twenty-three.

Ella   So it's him, Sophie, then you. You're the baby.

Dean   Thanks. Shame you ain't met Stacey, his girlfriend.

Ella   Press a 'hold'. Why?

Dean   She's nice, that's all.

Ella   Your brother's girlfriend? Shut up, I've got to revise.

Dean *looks at the book over* **Ella***'s shoulder.*

Dean 'Win A Million.' (*Sarky.*) Yeah, right.

Ella It's the name of a machine, fuckwit. Jackpot's two hundred and fifty quid.

Dean I've never seen anyone win anything like that.

Ella You've never seen anyone with this book.

Dean So how did you get it anyway?

Ella Mail order.

Dean Not tried it out yet?

Ella It only came this morning.

She takes the sunblock from **Dean**.

That's enough. I don't want to be too slippery.

She gets up, carrying her beach towel, sunblock and the book on cheating fruit machines.

Let's get started.

Dean *gets up, follows* **Ella**. *She approaches the café.*

Ella Think I can remember all the moves for 'Monte Carlo Cash Maze' – that's the machine they've got in the café.

Dean Fuck! Are you crazy? We can't try it in there. Ben's sure to be lurking about.

Ella Only think it's a laugh, won't he?

Dean Are you kidding? I'm dead.

Ella wraps the book in the towel.

Dean Look, why don't we go to the Firkin . . . or somewhere off his patch at least?

Ella Because I've revised for 'Monte Carlo Cash Maze'. If you're so worried you can be my lookout.

She goes into the café. **Dean** *follows, warily.* **Ella** *puts the wrapped book and sunblock on top of the fruit machine. She takes out her purse.*

Shit, I've hardly got any change left. Why didn't I check this morning?

Dean   I ain't got very much.

Ella   Never mind, just give us what you got.

Dean *reluctantly takes a few coins from his pocket.*

Ella   And the rest. Look, you'll get it back, and more, won't you?

Dean *takes out a handful of change.*

Ella   See that?

She indicates the lower right of the machine.

The cash pot. Twenty quid.

She readies herself, fingers poised at the controls.

Feed the baby.

Dean *puts a coin in.* **Ella** *presses a couple of buttons. Lights flash, sounds sound. A small amount of money is disgorged.*

Ella   This is the start of a new and profitable career!

Dean   You hope.

Dean *puts another coin in.*

Ella (*mutters*)   Nudge, nudge/nudge

Dean   /Shit!

Enter **Ben**. **Ben** *grabs hold of* **Dean**.

Ben   The kiosk is supposed to be *open*.

Dean   . . . Take it easy.

Ella (*mutters*)   Collect or gamble/ . . . er gamble.

Ella *presses a button.*

Ben   /*Take it easy!* That's your whole fucking problem.
Listen, you little cunt, you spend any more time pissing
about/ and you're out.

Ella   /Winning streak? Five pounds./ That'll do nicely.

Ella *plays on.*

Ben   /I won't be putting my arse on the line for you once
Mr Bayliss gets back. You're in for one hell of a shock, I'm
telling you.

Ella *sneaks a discreet peek in the towel-wrapped book, then plays on.*

Ben   Get yourself back over there and start shifting those
fucking ices, right now.

Ella   Collect or gamble . . .

Dean   Alright . . . no need to get heavy . . .

Ben   Heavy? I'll show you heavy, you miserable fuck.

He slams **Dean** *against the fruit machine. The machine starts paying
out ten quid.* **Ben** *and* **Dean** *stop to look at it.*

Oh, nice one!

He scoops out the coins. He hands them to **Ella** *who stuffs her pockets.
She is impatient to play again.* **Ben** *slouches against the machine, he
takes a little box from his pocket.*

Ella, what do you think about this? Thought I'd put the ring
in it. Do you think it looks alright as it is like, or did I ought
to wrap it up as well?

Ella *just wants him to go away.*

Ella   It's a nice box, Ben . . . er yeah, it's fine.

Ben   Yeah, I usually know the kind of stuff birds go for.

Ella   You did ought to wrap it though. Nice metallic
paper, little bow on top.

Ben   Metallic paper and bow, right, I'm on the case. (*To*
Dean.) What're you still hanging around for?

Dean *goes back to the ice-cream kiosk. He takes down the sign. He opens the kiosk, looks right and left, before starting to roll a joint on the serving hatch. In the café,* **Ella** *puts a coin in the fruit machine, starts playing.*

Ben   Knew you'd do that. Gonna pour all your winnings straight back in there, aren't you? You won't get that lucky again. Take a word from the wise, Ella, walk away while you're ahead.

Ella *is having trouble remembering the moves.*

Ella   Don't half fancy a cup of tea.

Ben   Same here. Ruby. Where the fuck is she? I don't believe this. Ruby!

He walks towards the back of the café. **Ella** *sneaks a quick look inside the book, presses a few buttons.* **Ben** *peers in the serving hatch. The machine starts to pay out again.* **Ben** *spins around.*

Fucking . . . (*Stops himself.*) Must be your lucky day, Ella.

Ella *collects up her winnings, thinks about having another go, but* **Ben** *is coming back over to her.*

Ella   About this much/milk

Ben *looks towards the serving hatch.*

Ben   /Ruby, you stupid slag.

Ella   . . . no sugar.

Ben   Tea-making isn't my department.

Ella *takes out a coin to start playing again, but* **Ben** *distracts her.*

Ben   Where's the fat tart got to? You know what the number one problem is in this organisation?

Ella   What?

Ben   Slackers.

He sprawls out at the table nearest the fruit machine. **Ella** *starts to play.*

Everywhere I look – fucking slackers, dossing around, having a laugh . . . I mean, what do you do – with people who don't have the work ethic? – apart from kick their bone-idle arses, at every opportunity.

Ella *loses her train of thought, not sure whether it's a 'hold' or a 'nudge' next.*

Ella   So you're the kick-arse man?

Ben   It's a dirty job but what the fuck. I'm a *grafter*, Ella. I believe it's possible to get somewhere . . . to be someone.

Ella   . . . and become the kicker not the kicked.

Ben   I hadn't looked at it like that – but yeah. The kicker not the kicked – like it.

Ella   Now me, I wouldn't be satisfied with that.

Ben   No? . . . So what do *you* want to be? . . . the person who kicks the kicker?

Ella   The person who *pays* someone else to kick the kicker.

Ben   And when's that gonna happen? When you're old enough to bloody retire, that's when.

Ella   I reckon on retiring at twenty-five.

Ben   Don't we all? So what do you do then?

Ella   I'm going to college.

Ben (*sceptical*)   Oh yeah.

Ella   To study leisure management.

Ben   I see. So that's what you're doing knocking about with our kid. Managing your leisure. Well, you couldn't pick a better teacher.

Ben *settles back lazily, watching* **Ella** *as she plays on the machine.*

Enter **Ruby** *from the left, stopping at the ice-cream kiosk.*

Dean   Hi, Rubes.

Ruby   Will Hamish be alright in there for another couple of days, do you reckon?

Dean   Yeah, no problem. So what you up to then – skiving off?

Ruby   Had to go to Waitrose, didn't I? For Mr Bayliss.

Dean   Bayliss! Shit – he's back?

Ruby   Yesterday, yeah. And he's had an accident see, so I've been doing his shopping.

Dean   An accident?

Ruby   I didn't like to ask him like . . . but Jake on the hoopla says he fell. You know, *in there*.

Ruby *leaves* **Dean**, *goes into the café.*

Ben   Well, look who it is.

Ella *is concentrating on the machine. Lots of lights flash.*

Ella   Lucky Bonus???

Ben *gets up, goes over to* **Ruby**. **Ella** s*neaks a quick look at the book.*

Ella (*mutters*)   . . . check the sum on offer and . . . (*She turns over a couple of pages.*)

Ben   What have I told you about *reliefs*, Ruby? – read my lips – You need to go somewhere, you ask someone to relieve you.

Ruby   Ain't no one to relieve me, is there? Since Naomi/ left . . .

Ben   Naomi – natural-born slacker/

Dean   Ices!

Ella (*on the fruit machine, softly*)   nudge/ . . .

Ruby   /Don't think I don't know what goes on! Don't think you'll get rid of me and all!

Ben   Ruby . . .

Ruby   Don't 'Ruby' me. You're . . . you're *oily* . . . that's what you are. I wasn't on a relief, I was shopping. For Mr Bayliss.

Dean   Ice creams!

Ben   Fucking . . . !

Ruby   Didn't you know? Come back yesterday he did.

Ben   Oh . . . oh, right . . . that's great, yeah . . . look forward to seeing the old . . . to seeing him, yeah. Yeah, erm, we'd like a couple of teas, please, Ruby. One with, one without.

Ruby *stands her ground a moment, then goes behind the counter.* **Ben** *goes back to* **Ella** *who is carefully playing the machine. For a moment he resists the temptation to tamper, and then he presses nudge.* **Ella** *starts.*

Ella   Shit!

Ben   You've got to have a bit of a knack with these things. Right, let's just clear this little lot.

Ella   No!

Ben *presses a few buttons.*

Ella   Oh, fuck.

Ben *holds his hand out to* **Ella** *for money.*

Ella   Use your own.

Ben *takes a coin from his pocket, puts it in the machine. He presses some buttons.*

Ben   Two bars. That's looking promising . . .

He presses more buttons.

Nearly. Hang in there. (*Press.*) This is looking more like it. (*Press.*) Almost got three bars there, see that?

Ella *goes outside.* **Ben** *doesn't notice. He puts another coin in the slot. He plays on.* **Ella** *goes up to* **Dean**'s *kiosk.*

Dean   Made a million?

Ella   Fuck off. (*A beat.*) Ben's a sad fuck.

Dean (*passing her the joint*)   You've noticed.

He opens the door to the kiosk.

Coming in?

Ella *walks down to the beach, sits down.*

Dean (*softly*)   Fuck.

He looks around. He leaves the kiosk, joins **Ella**.

Just you keep your eyes peeled for Ben or Mr Bayliss.

In the café, **Ben** *finally notices* **Ella** *has gone. Behind the hatch,* **Ruby** *combs her hair.*

Ella   Who's Mr Bayliss?

Dean   He's like almost my uncle . . . well, it's a bit more complicated . . .

Ella   So why do you call him mister, if he's almost your uncle?

Dean   Like I said, it's complicated.

Ella *stretches out on the shingle to sunbathe.* **Dean** *crouches beside her, not wanting to sit in case of tar. She takes out a bottle of nail varnish.*

Ella   Metallic green. Nice, innit?

Ella *starts to varnish her toenails. In the café,* **Ben** *collects up* **Ella**'s *sunblock and towel and finds the book.*

Ruby   Was it two teas you said?

Ben *is engrossed in the book. He props it up against the machine. He puts money in the slot.*

Ben (*reading*)   'Check the cash pot.' – Twenty quid. Right.

Ben *puts more money in the machine.*

On the beach, **Dean** *sees his trainer has got tar on it.*

Dean   Oh fuck.

Dean *scrapes at the tar with a piece of seaweed.*

Ben *turns the page, continues to play the machine, getting more engrossed and excited.*

Ben   Nudge.

He consults the book. **Ruby** *brings two teas over.*

Ruby   What're you doing?

Ben   Look at this, it's a book that shows you how to win every time. (*Reading.*) 'Lucky Bonus. Choose one of the two cash prizes shown.'

Ben *consults the book, does the moves.* **Ruby** *watches.*

Ruby   Is that legal?

Ben   I'm just testing it, Ruby.

Ruby   Yeah?

Ben   It belongs to that girl who's been kicking around with Dean. Do you know her? Is she a mate of yours?

Ruby   No . . . Naomi was my friend . . .

Ben   Look, I was sad to let her go, right. But it had to be done. Pubes in the coffee just ain't hygienic.

Ben *is pouring money into the machine like there's no tomorrow.*

On the beach, **Dean** *takes his trainer off, puts it down beside* **Ella**.

Ella   Urh, hot cheese!

Ella *hurls the trainer down the beach.* **Dean** *hops after it.*

In the café, **Ben** *indicates the page.*

Ben   Just a couple of nudges and it'll pay out big time.

Ruby   Are you gonna give the money back?

Ben   . . . Well, of course . . . I'm . . . going to report the problem to the manufacturers . . . Ruby, have you left any of those chocolate chip cookies?

Ruby   . . . Dunno, maybe.

Ben   It's hard to concentrate on an empty stomach, you know what I'm saying . . .

Ruby *goes behind the hatch.* **Ben** *presses the buttons on the machine.*

Ben   Yes, yes, yes. (*A beat.*) Fuck!

On the beach, **Dean** *returns with water dripping from his trainer.*

Ella   Sit down.

Dean   No fucking way.

In the café, **Ben** *looks at the book.* **Ruby** *starts to return.*

Ruby (*pleased*)   No cookies left.

Ben   Look at this. *Look at this!* (*Reading.*) 'If, at this stage, the machine doesn't offer you the chance of winning the jackpot, then it may well have been rigged so that the jackpot cannot be won.

Enter **Edwin**, *standing in the doorway on his crutches.*

Ben, *oblivious, kicks the machine.*

Ben   That's fifteen quid I've just lost in this fucking thing! Fuck that crook Bayliss! Fuck him.

Edwin (*matter-of-factly*)   My office, Benjamin. A quick word.

Ben *stares at* **Edwin** *in horror.*

Ruby   Good morning, Mr Bayliss.

Edwin   Morning, Ruby.

Exit **Edwin** *and* **Ben** (*looking like a condemned man*).

Pleased, **Ruby** *helps herself to a slice of cake from the counter.*

Blackout.

Scene Four

Ella *and* **Dean** *are in the ice-cream kiosk.* **Dean** *opens a new box of Flakes, lets* **Ella** *choose one. He ducks down out of sight and strokes her with it.*

Ella   I have to go *now*, don't I? Ain't got no choice in the matter.

Dean   P'raps he won't notice.

Ella   Won't notice. Shit, Dean, how can he fail to notice a full set of replacement double glazing?

Dean   You could dirty 'em up a bit . . . and maybe get some thick curtains . . .

Ella   He's still gonna notice when the bill arrives.

Dean   So how come the double glazing people didn't get your letter cancelling the windows?

Ella   Perhaps they did. Perhaps they just ignored it.

Dean   Can't trust anyone, can you?

Ella   Course you can't. But it shouldn't have mattered. I'd planned it all so careful. Me and Stefan were gonna take the free flight last week. Wouldn't have mattered then, if dad had still got double-glazed. I'd be in Hollywood now.

If only I'd checked all the small print. Why didn't I notice you can't take the flights 'til fucking September?

Dean   So you've got to stay here 'til then?

Ella   Fuck no! Dad'll be back on Monday.

Dean   Can't you talk to him? Explain it was like a mistake . . . or something?

Ella   He don't listen to me. Not since Sandra moved in. She only has to point her turbo tits in his direction and he goes deaf on me. No, I gotta leave town this weekend, for definite.

Dean   Are you going to London?

Ella   I might.

Dean *pops back up.*

Dean   To live with that Stefan?

Ella   He doesn't . . . have like a permanent address at the moment . . .

Dean   He's dossing?

Ella   He's been sleeping on a mate's floor . . . since he lost his job.

Dean   I don't get what you see in that bloke, Ella. I mean, he's a pervert . . .

Ella   He's not!

Ella *pushes* **Dean** *down out of sight. He strokes her with the Flake again.*

Dean   You said he wears women's knickers.

Ella   . . . But if he can take this job with his uncle's company, we'll get to meet everyone. Johnny Depp, Brad Pitt . . .

Dean *pops back up.*

Dean   Uma Thurman?

Ella   Everyone.

Dean   All I'm saying is, is it really worth leaving your friends, and living with some pervy chef just so you meet famous people?

Ella   Yeah.

Dean   . . . Yeah, if I could meet Uma Thurman, yeah . . .

Enter **Ruby**.

Ruby   Dean!

Ella *pulls her jeans up.*

Dean   Fancy a Mivvy, Rubes?

Ruby   Can you get Hamish out for me?

Dean   You wanna take him now?

Ruby   No . . . I just want to see him a minute . . .

Dean *disappears from sight to rummage in the freezer.*

Dean   What box did we use?

Ruby   A Rolo lolly one.

Dean   Shit, it's right at the bottom, under the new box of Magnums.

Ella   Magnums, yeah. Give us one then.

Ruby   You've gotta pay for it. You can't just eat ice creams whenever you feel like it. The place would go out of business if you did that, see?

Ella *gives* **Ruby** *a look.* **Dean** *emerges with a Rolo lolly box, hands it through the hatch to* **Ruby**. **Ruby** *opens the box, inside is something wrapped in tissue. She unwraps it a little.* **Ella** *tries to peer into the box.* **Ruby** *tenderly strokes the something inside the tissue, with her finger.*

Ella   Urh. What is it?

Dean   Frozen hamster.

Ella   It's dead?

Dean (*sarkily*)   No.

Ruby *nods.*

Ruby   Put him back.

Dean *takes the box containing Hamish and puts it back in the freezer.*

Ella   What you keeping it for?

Ruby   I need to think about what to do. I don't have a garden, so I can't really bury him . . . but I can't just chuck him in the dustbin . . . it's not right.

Ella   What about one of those recycling bins, then?

Dean   Drop him off the pier – burial at sea.

Ruby   I just want to do the right thing, that's all . . . Maybe I should ask Mr Bayliss.

Ruby *heads back to the café.*

Ella   So he's a hamster expert and all – your Mr Bayliss? It's not just the goldfish. If he's so into animals, maybe I should ask him about our dog's bad breath.

Dean (*interrupting*)   No . . . don't do that! Whatever you do, Ella. He hates dogs. Because of his leg, see?

Ella   No . . . What, did a dog bite his leg or something?

Dean   *Mauled* him, yeah. I was talking to Madame Zara. Massive great German shepherd dog. Chewed it through to the bone.

Ella   Urh.

Dean   Chewed his leg half off. She saw it all in her crystal ball.

Ella   No . . .

Dean   Prison guard dog . . .

Ella   He was in prison?

Dean   Came out yesterday.

Ella   What he do?

Dean   Got into a mess with his taxes.

Ella   Like he didn't pay 'em?

Dean   Something like that, yeah.

Ella   Bit of a crook, is he?

Dean   Only it wasn't his fault . . . he just took the rap.

Ella   . . . Oh shit . . .

Dean   Madame Zara says she saw the whole thing coming –

Ella *starts searching for something.*

Dean   Yeah, her spirit guide warned her –

Ella (*interrupting*)   Dean, have you seen my book?

Dean   What? Not since we were in the café.

Ella   Fuck, I must've left it there.

She leaves the kiosk, goes into the café. She sees the book is no longer on top of the fruit machine. **Ruby** *is eating a muffin.* **Ella** *walks over to her.*

Do you know where Ben's got to?

Ruby   He's with Mr Bayliss.

Ella   Oh . . .

Ruby   He's got your book.

Ella   My what?

Ruby   Your book on cheating.

Ella   I don't know what you're on about.

Ruby *shrugs.* **Dean** *comes into the café.*

Dean   Have you got it?

Ella *motions to* **Dean** *to shut up.*

Ruby (*without looking up*)   Mr Bayliss has got it.

Dean   Oh fuck. Now you really need to go to America . . . like tomorrow or something.

Ella   What? I told you it ain't that simple. I gotta make some money –

Dean   *Mr Bayliss has got your book!*

Ella   Then I'll have to persuade him to give it back.

Ruby *looks up.*

Dean   Not a good idea.

Ella   What's with you? You're scared of some bloke with only one and a half legs?

Dean   You don't understand . . . Mr Bayliss is *connected.*

Ella   Connected? To what?

Enter **Ben**.

Ruby *gives him a black look, disappears behind the kitchen hatch.*

Ben (*to* **Dean**)   Delivery's arrived. So shift yourself!

Exit **Dean**.

Ella . . . you're looking at a dead man.

Ella   So that's what the smell is.

Ben   You don't know how lucky you are it was me he caught with it, not you.

Ella   You what?

Ben   Your book, Ella . . .

Ella   What/ book?

Ben   /the book that was wrapped in your towel, the book that was beside your sunblock.

Ella   What towel? Sunblock? I was helping Dean in the kiosk. They probably belong to some daytripper . . .

Ben   He'll only believe I wasn't the one trying to empty his machines if I give him a name.

Ella   So you gave him mine?

Ben   I put my fucking arse on the line for you, Ella.

Ella   Violins are playing.

Ben   Gotta give him a name by the end of week. I said I'm investigating . . .

Ella   You wonder where somebody could've got a book like that, don't you? And whether they were getting rich by using it . . .

Enter **Dean** *carrying a pile of ice-cream boxes to the kiosk.*

Ben   I doubt it. The machine's fixed so you can't win the jackpot . . .

Dean *dumps the boxes, exits.*

Ella   Oh, so you tried it then?

Ben   Well, I/ had to test it.

Ella   /Did you have much luck?

Ben   Er . . . a bit like . . . but I can't really see how you . . . how a person could make serious money like that. I mean, it says in the book you can't clean a machine out. It's always gonna swipe back a big cut of your winnings.

Ella   Maybe . . . the person wouldn't just concentrate on fruit machines. Maybe if they were a real *entrepreneur* . . . they'd know other ways to make money . . .

Ben   Like what?

Ella   Like they'd see a place like this . . .

Ella *goes outside the café.* **Ben** *follows.*

Ben   . . . Like this café, right . . .

Ella   This café, the arcades, all the kiosks/ on the pier and prom . . .

Ben   /The whole fucking Bayliss empire, yeah . . .

Ella   . . . as full of money-making opportunities.

Ben   Yeah, if you're Mr Bayliss, sitting back and watching the cash roll in.

Ella   King Slacker.

Ben   He doesn't lift a fucking finger.

Enter **Dean** *laden with boxes again.* **Ella** *and* **Ben** *follow him back to the ice-cream kiosk.*

Ella   But it's not so hot being the kick-arse man?

Ben   All I'm saying is there's no chance of making any money here . . . unless you're Mr Bayliss.

Ella   You reckon?

Ben   Dean, you lazy piece of pond-life, get those lollies out of the sun. As you may have noticed, Ella, I'm a man who's motivated. If I could see a way of making something for myself, I'd be double mad for it.

Dean *starts loading the kiosk's freezer with lolly boxes.*

Ella   You'd be the new Richard Branson . . .

Ben   Only I wouldn't go calling my business empire 'Virgin'. I mean, that must've made people wonder about the geezer . . . But yeah, I want to be a self-made man . . .

Ella   What's stopping you?

Ben   Money. You need money to make money.

Ella   Look around you . . . all those people on the beach, every one with money in their pockets . . .

Ben   Yeah, well, none of it's coming my way, is it?

Ella   Cos you ain't got nothing to sell them. Look at them
– frittering it on ice cream, burgers, beers, arcade games,
sticks of rock, palm readings, postcards of bums and tits . . .
Any old shit really, to convince themselves they've had the
whole seaside experience.

Ben   Yeah, but you've got to buy the rock or the postcards
off someone, and you've got to spend out hundreds on stock
before you start making any profits.

Ella   I can see you've thought about this . . . but what if
you sold something that never ran out?

Ben   Everything runs out eventually.

Ella   Not if you only *loan* it.

Ben   . . . Like . . . deckchairs. Bayliss has got a deckchair
man and it's a shitty job – lots of old grunts who won't pay
up for the pleasure of parking their flabby arses.

Ella   Or boat trips. On a boat trip, the punter coughs up
the readies before they get to leave dry land.

Ben   There's already a bloke on the lower esplanade
selling boat trips.

Ella   Yeah, I went on one once. It was shite. Nothing to
look at but sea. I mean, you can see that from the fucking
beach. Then I got talking to this old fisherman . . . asked
him how come he could stand the boredom of being stuck in
the middle of the fucking ocean for hours on end. Well, he
goes on about the red sunsets, the silvery dawn, mournful
cries of the gulls – it still didn't sound much of a party to
me. Then he mentioned the dolphins . . .

Dean   I can't get all the Feasts in the freezer.

Ben   Sit on the fucking lid. (*To* **Ella**.) The dolphins yeah?
What dolphins?

Ella   One day he's fishing a . . . nautical mile or so from
the end of the pier, and suddenly there's like these two
dolphins jumping and playing just in front of his boat. Well,

he drops anchor and he sits there and watches as they do somersaults, walk on their tails, and balance fish on their noses . . . Then he remembers, that the dolphins from the old aquarium were released into the sea a couple of years back . . . as part of some conservation thing . . .

Ben   I saw about that in the papers.

Dean   Smartie and Poppy, that were their names.

Ella   Yeah, so he took me out there – and there they were, – Smartie and Poppy – performing their whole act a mile or so offshore.

Ben   I bet Mr Bayliss would give his good leg to know that. He's into fish, like.

Ella   Dolphins aren't fish . . . But, well, I thought about it and realised there's a lot of money to be made from selling boat trips to see the dolphins . . .

Ben   Well, yeah . . .

Ella   Only I don't have a boat . . . and I'm leaving town soon.

Ben   I still think it's a shame you won't be here for Sophie's party.

Ella   There's a slim chance I might be . . .

Ben   Yeah? . . . Yeah, if you ask me, it's a shame you've got to leave at all. I mean, I think you've really got something there. A first-class business opportunity.

Ella   . . . Even if I ran the boat trips for a while like, and then handed the whole thing over to someone else . . . .

Ben   It's worth thinking about.

Ella   Yeah . . . but who'd I leave it to?

Ben   Well . . . I'm not saying I'd be interested for definite yet but it's a thought, isn't it?

Ella   You and me working together . . . I don't know . . .

Ben   I can really see us making a go of this dolphin thing . . . making some serious dosh, Ella.

Ella   Well, I couldn't do anything about setting it up unless I had a boat . . . And somewhere where people could book their boat trips . . .

Ben   What you need is a kiosk on the prom. You'd have to rent one from Mr Bayliss.

Ella   A kiosk, right. And are there any available?

Ben   Oh yeah, there's quite a few standing empty.

Ella   Business is slow round here?

Ben   . . . Er, no, it's because of the rent increases. There's been some big ones recently . . .

Dean   Not half.

Ella   How much is it to rent a kiosk?

Ben   Depends.

Ella   On?

Ben   Er . . . well, I'm in charge of rent collection, see . . . And if I was in on the whole deal . . . I could make sure the rent was very reasonable . . .

Ella   . . . I'm still not sure I want to go into partnership, Ben. This *is* my idea, after all.

Ben   I'd been thinking about something along the same lines for quite a while, hadn't I, Dean?

Ella   Bollocks. You didn't know the dolphins even fucking existed, 'til I opened my big mouth.

Ben   No, it was going to be seabird tours/ but it's the same principle.

Ella   /What! Who'd pay to look at a poxy seagull?

Ben   Anyway, if you tried to set up without me, you'd find the rent far too high . . . and subject to regular increases.

Dean　Ben even put Madame Zara's rent up after Mr Bayliss went inside.

Ben　The old crone's always getting aggro from dissatified punters. Catch her on a bad day and her predictions are all doom and gloom. That's not what people like to hear, is it? She's the main reason we're having to get security cameras.

Ella　So I need to see Mr Bayliss about getting a kiosk. And what about the boat?

Ben　Yeah, that's a point . . . and who's gonna skipper it?

Dean (*popping up behind the hatch*)　I'm up for that.

Ben　When've you ever driven a boat?

Dean　Butlin's. Remember.

Ben　This isn't a pedalo. It's gonna have an outboard/ motor.

Dean　/Cool!

Ella　And oars so you can row right up close to the dolphins without scaring them.

Dean　It's not gonna be really difficult or anything. I mean, you don't get any box junctions or reversing round the corners in the sea, do you?/ All the passengers'll have life jackets on anyway.

Ella　/He's right, you know.

Ben　So we just need to get our hands on a boat.

Ella　We need to rent one, yeah.

Ben　And where are we going to get the money . . .

Ella *and* **Dean** *look at* **Ben**.

Blackout.

Scene Five

Ruby *is behind the hatch, in the café.*

Ella *and* **Dean** *are in the ice-cream kiosk with a copy of* The Aquarist *magazine.*

Dean   OK, what's this?

Ella   Calico fantail.

Dean   Yep. This one?

Ella   Bristol shubunkin.

Dean   This?

Ella   Metallic veiltail suffering from fin rot.

Dean   Goldfish suck. All they're good at is dying. How's Shane getting on with the dolphins?

Ella   They're looking pretty good. But you've gotta remember not to take the public too near . . . so they don't hear the motors, or see them too close-up.

Dean   No problem.

Ella   Shane's programming them so they'll swim around a bit on their own, and you'll have a remote control to reposition them with after each trip.

Dean   The thing is . . . Ben wants to go on the first trip . . . why'd you tell him they were real dolphins, Ella?

Ella   Cos he'd never have put up the money for the boat if he thought there was any risk involved. Ben doesn't have any *imagination*, Dean.

Dean   Not like us, eh? We've got plenty of imagination, haven't we? . . . Which reminds me, there's a new box of Flakes arrived . . .

Ella   Listen to me. This dolphin venture's important, Dean. It's gonna get you and me on that plane to Hollywood.

Dean   Yeah!

Ella   The dolphins should be ready for a trial run on Saturday. Take Ben along. If they're good enough to fool the punters, they'll fool him, no bother. You could take Sophie too – on her birthday – be a nice treat for her. And as you've still got to learn to manage the boat on the sea, you might as well practise on your no-good family.

Dean   Driving the boat's a doddle, Ella. What you need to worry about is getting a kiosk out of old Bayliss. That's gonna be the hard part.

Ella   Well, shut up and let me revise then!

Ella *goes back to the magazine.*

Edwin *and* **Ben** *enter the café talking.* **Edwin** *is still on crutches.*

Edwin   . . . Get Dean to give you a hand with it . . .

Ben *goes across to the ice-cream kiosk, indicates to* **Dean** *to follow him.*

Ruby   Afternoon, Mr Bayliss.

Ben *and* **Dean** *exit.*

Edwin   Hallo, Ruby.

Edwin *looks at the fish.*

Ruby (*tense*)   They're alright, aren't they?

Edwin   Bronzino still seems a little . . . bloated.

Ruby   Perhaps I have been overfeeding them . . .

Edwin   You've not still been feeding them, since I've been back?

Dean *and* **Ben** *enter carrying the back wall of a kiosk. As the scene continues they fetch the other walls and the front, which bears the sign 'Scampi Sam's Seafood'.* **Dean** *and* **Ben** *prise the sign off and discard it.*

Ruby   Oh yes.

Edwin   Then they've been having two meals a day . . .

Ruby   You didn't tell me to stop . . . and they still keep coming up for it . . .

Edwin   Don't you know you can kill goldfish by overfeeding?

Ruby   Oh. Sorry, Mr Bayliss. (*Pause.*) Mr Bayliss, do you think I could talk to you about something . . .

Edwin   If it's about your wages there'll be my usual autumnal review.

Ruby   No, no it's not that . . .

Edwin   If it's the situation regarding Naomi . . . I think in the circumstances, Benjamin's decision to dismiss her was probably the correct one.

Ruby   Ben only sacked Naomi because she . . . she . . .

Edwin   Because her . . . standards of hygiene were perhaps not up to the level required? General and personal cleanliness are essential in the catering trade, Ruby . . .

Ruby   I've been doing my best to keep everything spotless . . .

Edwin   I'm sure you have. But as an added precaution, now that I'm back, I'm going to ask Benjamin to add a thorough inspection of all food outlets to his nightly round. You can't be too careful in matters of hygiene, can you, Ruby?

Ruby   No, Mr Bayliss.

Edwin *taps the glass of the fish tank.*

Edwin   Hmmm, Bronzino's decidedly sluggish . . .

Ruby   I could crank the aerator up a bit. Give him a few more bubbles.

Edwin   Do we still have the same vet?

Ruby   Mr Hall?

Edwin   Excellent man.

Ruby   . . . Er, he *did himself.* It was the same week our Punch and Judy man did it and all. I mean, there's talk . . .

Edwin   There's always talk.

Ruby   . . . Mr Bayliss, what I wanted to ask you about is Hamish, my hamster.

Ella *comes into the café.*

Edwin   Ella, isn't it?

Ella's *attention is with the fish.*

Ella   Red-caps. The bigger one looks a bit iffy. Swim bladder trouble, do you reckon?

Edwin   I hope not. But his scales are sticking out rather . . .

Ella   Could be dropsy or he might just've been overfed.

Edwin *looks at* **Ruby**.

Ella   It's a common mistake, overfeeding goldfish. But the results can be very serious.

Edwin   Yes, indeed.

Ella   Do you have any coldwater fish tonic?

Edwin   I'm afraid not . . .

Ella   I'll bring mine over, if you like. Just two drops in a tank this size . . . well, I'm sure you know that.

Edwin   You keep fish?

Ella   I've a few koi and some marines . . . just to keep my hand in.

Edwin *sits down.* **Ella** *follows suit.*

Edwin Benjamin tells me you're interested in renting one of my kiosks . . .

Ella Yeah, maybe. I mean, depending on your terms. I've been looking at kiosks at several places . . . shopping around, y'know.

Edwin Very sensible . . . you might find a cheaper deal elsewhere, though you won't find a more profitable site than on the pier and my section of the prom.

Ella I'd only want to rent it on a temporary basis to begin with . . . say for a fortnight –

Edwin I'm sorry, I only deal in seasonal lets. If you want it, you've got to take the lease from now until September. Two months rent in advance. That's the deal.

Ella That's a pretty heavy investment . . .

Edwin It's a big commitment, yes, but I presume you've thought it through properly . . .

Ella I have, yeah . . . and I'm confident my plan has real money-making potential. Of course, I'd love to be able to give you more details at this stage, but as this is such an original, and potentially . . . er . . .

Edwin Lucrative?

Ella Extremely lucrative idea, I can't reveal any more information about it until we've signed the agreement for the kiosk rental.

Edwin I understand.

Ella I knew you would, Mr Bayliss.

Edwin Edwin.

Ella But Edwin, I . . . feel I ought to be able to trust you . . .

Edwin As long as you pay me your two months' in advance, it's no concern of mine what you use the kiosk for.

Ella   The thing is . . . I mean, supposing I pay you one month in advance, with a guaranteed share of profits . . .

Edwin   My terms aren't open to negotiation.

He gets up.

Take it or leave it, Ella.

Blackout.

Scene Six

Late evening. **Ella***'s kiosk is assembled now. A sign on it reads 'Trips to see the dolfins. Ask here.'* **Dean** *is very drunk, beside the kiosk.*

Dean (*shouting, hysterical*)   Very funny! Very fucking funny. I'm laughing. Ha ha ha. Ha ha ha. Come on then! Fucking come on!!!

Enter **Ben***. He grabs hold of* **Dean***, trying to prevent him going to fight someone, off.*

Ben   Leave it!

Dean *shouts at someone unseen, off.*

Dean   You're all talk, aren't yer? . . . And . . . and . . . your bird's a shit shagger!

Ben   Shut it.

Dean   Did you see that scrote Jordan coming on to Ella?

Ben   Where is Ella?

Dean   I kicked him in the head. Did you see me?

Ben   Have you seen her?

Dean   Did you see him coming on to Stacey? I told him he was dead. You'll have him, I said. You'll fucking have him.

Ben   I've told you it's over with Stacey. I mean, she's a top bird and everything . . . but, well, I need my freedom, don't I?

Dean   You still can't let her disgrace you with that pisshole. People still *think* she's your bird . . . They think she's shitting on you, bro.

Ben *grabs hold of* **Dean** *again.*

Ben   I want you to go home, go home now, got it?

Dean   Can't I stay at yours?

Ben   No.

Dean   Mum'll kill me when she gets in and sees the mess.

Ben   I said go home, Dean. Now.

Dean   Ben, I . . .

Ben   Home!

Dean   Ha, ha, ha. Ben, I love you, man.

He tries to hug **Ben**.

I fucking love you.

Ben   Fuck Off Home! Look, I've gotta do my round, check security on the pier. If you're still here when I get back . . .

Dean   I'm going. I'm going.

Exit **Ben**.

Dean (*to himself*)   I'm going.

Ella *stands up in the kiosk swigging a Foster's Ice.*

Ella   Dean?

Dean *turns round.*

Ella   He gone?

Dean *pukes.*

Ella Urh.

Dean *wipes his mouth.*

Dean Killer party, eh, Ella? (*Studying his puke, unsteadily.*)
Look, no peas or carrots . . . that's a first, that is. Getting too
old for all this debauchery, aren't I?

Ella Can't hold your Alcopop – baby.

Dean I kicked that Jordan right in the head. Did you see
me?

Ella *comes out of the kiosk, wearing her party dress. She looks at the
sign. She shoves* **Dean***, he loses his balance, steps in the puke.*

Dean Shit.

Ella Dolphin's got a PH in it.

Dean Yeah, I know, alright? I know . . . That's why I left
big gaps between the letters. So I could stick them in when I
find where they go.

He wipes his foot on the pebbles.

Me best pair of Nikes.

Ella And I said put 'Enquire Within' – sounds nicer.

Ella *swigs from the bottle.*

Dean It's not put anyone off. We're all booked up. You
should've made Ben rent a bigger boat. He's such a fucking
skinflint, my brother . . .

Ella You said the practice run went OK, 's'afternoon?

Dean No probs. Piss easy, innit?

Ella So why did Ben show up at yours soaking wet?

Dean He went for a swim. Just dived in before I could
stop him. Said he was gonna swim with 'Poppy and
Smartie'. Said it would be therapeutic – cure his backache
and that.

Ella   He didn't get near them?

Dean   No – I got to the remote control in time, pressed 'reset', sent them zooming out to sea. Told Ben they were shy like.

Ella   He believed you?

Dean   No worries. I couldn't believe the speed of those dolphins when I pushed the button. Took off like bloody missiles they did.

Ella   Yeah, knew I could rely on Shane.

Ella *walks down the beach.*

Dean   But you're not . . . I mean, you're definitely not shagging him?

Ella   I told you I'm not. Anyway he's with Leanne – my best mate.

Dean   Don't think I've met her.

Ella   Don't see her much now, do I?

Dean   Cos you've shagged her bloke?

Ella   Cos she's got a baby. (*Pause.*) I hate babies. They smell.

Ella *lies down on the pebbles, flat on her back.* **Dean** *looks at her legs.*

Dean   Yeah . . . Yeah, I don't like babies. You know . . . you know, Ella, me and you've got a lot in common . . .

Ella   Both pissed as farts.

Dean   Yeah! Been thinking . . . we oughta team up or something . . . you and me . . .

Dean *moves to touch* **Ella***'s thigh, doesn't dare.* **Ella** *doesn't notice.*

. . . cos you're a top bird . . . and we're like . . . like soulmates or something . . .

He almost touches her thigh, pulls back.

And you're really foxy . . .

He touches her thigh. **Ella** *sits up, thumps him, hard.*

Ow!

Ella You're perverted, Dean.

Ben (*off*) Ella!

Ella Shit . . .

Dean Big brother's not a happy bunny.

Ella Why didn't you fucking tell me? I mean, I knew your Sophie works in shop. But it would have to be a fucking jewellers.

Dean The wrong fucking birthstone . . . and it wasn't gold neither. Twenty-five quid! Man, you kill me, you do. You're just the foxiest babe.

Ella *kicks him.*

Enter **Ben**, *walking past the café.*

Ella Shhhh. Keep still.

Ben Ella!

Dean *and* **Ella** *watch* **Ben** *look in the kiosk.*

Dean Reckon he fancies another flake?

Ella Shhh.

Enter **Ruby**, *long coat over her nightie.*

Ben (*jumpy*) Shit. Ruby . . . You give me quite a turn like. For a minute, I thought you were old Eliza Bayliss come back . . .

Ruby What . . . have you seen her?

Ben Old Eliza Bayliss, walking along the prom, her dress dripping wet, seaweed and barnacles in her hair . . .

Ruby Don't . . .

Ben What you doing wandering about in your nightie, anyway?

Ella *creeps up the beach, treading carefully among the pebbles.* **Dean** *watches.*

Ruby . . . Er . . . I want to talk to Dean about something.

Ben You and Dean? Well, I'd never have guessed. Dean! Dean, here's Ruby in her negligee, looking for you, bro!

Dean *stumbles after* **Ella**, **Ben** *turns round to see them caught out in the open.*

Ella Ben! I've been looking everywhere for you.

Ruby *looks in the ice-cream kiosk.*

Ben Oh have you now?

Ruby (*quietly to* **Dean**)   Can I see Hamish?

Dean *burps.*

Ruby I couldn't sleep. I've started making him a proper coffin.

Dean *and* **Ruby** *go into the kiosk, open the freezer, start taking out boxes. While* **Ben** *is temporarily distracted, watching them,* **Ella** *starts to sneak off.* **Ben** *sees her, grabs her arm and drags her down the beach.*

Ella Ow. 'ere, careful.

Ben Thought you'd give me the slip, did you?

Ella When?

Ben At Sophie's fucking party!

Ella What? I just went outside to . . . look at the stars . . .

Ben (*looking at the sky*)   – It's cloudy.

Ella So I came back in again, and you'd gone.

Ben   . . . looking for you, you crooked little —

Ella   I realised I'd made a dreadful mistake over the ring, and —

Ben   You can say that again.

Ella   Pearl is Sophie's birthstone, not topaz. I mean, what a stupid, stupid mistake. I'm always getting confused about the names and colours of stones. I always get garnets muddled up with opals, and can't tell peridots from zirconias —

Ben   Yeah right, look, Ella —

Ella   I don't know how you can be so understanding. It was supposed to be a special present for your sister.

Ben   It was supposed to be gold.

Ella   What/ . . . what are you saying? Wait a minute. It *is* gold.

Ruby   Hamish.

Ben   On the surface maybe . . .

Ella   That ring's hallmarked. Inside, in the middle . . .

Ben   It says 'Made In Taiwan'.

Ella   Oh my God! Honestly? Shit. Look, you must let me give you your money back.

Ben   Well, yeah, I —

Ella   I insist, Ben. A full refund. I feel really terrible . . . and when I think that my dad . . . God, it's awful.

Ben   Your dad? Your dad what?

Ella   Gave me that ring for my eighteenth! What a cheap bastard! I know you shouldn't say things like that about your dad but — he's a complete crook . . .

Ben   Dean told me he sells insurance.

Ella   Well, exactly.

Ben   I see, so we're not talking 'Man from the Pru' type insurance then, right?

Ella   . . . Er, that's right . . .

Ben   He's *connected*, is that what you're saying?

Ella   Connected . . . yeah, yeah, he is.

Ben   Knows some pretty heavy-type people?

Ella   Yeah . . . like when I was born I had this big gangland christening . . .

Ben   Don Corleone was your godfather, yeah, same here. Like Bayliss and the Krays were this close. (*Pause.*) So you're gonna give me back my twenty-five quid?

Ella *sits down on the beach.*

Ella   Of course. As soon as I have it.

Ben   Shit! You've spent it?

Ella   Invested it, in our dolphin-watching venture.

Ben   Since *I* paid for the boat and the rent of the kiosk . . . in what *exactly* did you invest it.

Ella   Stock.

Ben   Stock?

Ben *sits down beside her.*

In the kiosk, **Dean** *pops up with a Flake.*

Dean   Ella!

Ella *sticks a finger up at* **Dean** *behind* **Ben**'s *back.*

Ella   Look, we don't start the boat trips until tomorrow, and the first two are already fully booked. This is the time to start talking expansion. To start thinking of having a second kiosk to sell souvenirs.

Ben   So you've spent *my* twenty-five quid on what exactly?

Ella   Fluffy dolphins, squeaky dolphins, dolphin snow-scenes – you know, shake 'em up . . .

Ben   And it snows. Right.

Ella   Postcards . . . of dolphins. Got them cheap from a shop in town. He couldn't shift 'em after the dolphinarium closed. Dolphin mugs, dolphin keyrings, inflatable dolphins . . .

Ben   So when will I get my money back?

Ella   The stock arrives tomorrow. One of those overnight-delivery things. As it starts selling, which it will, like hot cakes, I'll start putting the profit on one side for you. Double your money in a fortnight.

Ben   Right . . .

Ruby   One last stroke.

Ella   All I need now is that second kiosk.

Ben   What's wrong with the one we've got?

Ella   Nothing. But like I said think expansion. I *could* sell souvenirs from our little kiosk, but only a few at a time. We wouldn't be able to display all our stock at once. Now if we had one of those big kiosks on the pier where people can walk round and pick out what they want . . .

Ben   I can't afford the rent for one of those.

Ella   We could use the advance-booking money from the boat trips plus the first couple of weeks profit from the souvenirs, that's if you could wait a fortnight for your money back.

Ben   My money back doubled you said.

Ella   Of course. If we don't expand and quickly, someone else'll spot the gap in the market and get in first. We'll be running the boat trips – doing all the graft and some other bugger'll be cashing in.

Dean   Let me.

Ben   The problem is, Ella, there's only three of those big kiosks on the pier, and they're all taken for the season.

Ella   Nobody thinking of moving on?

Ben   No.

Ella   All doing well?

Ben   I ain't heard no complaints.

Ruby   Gently.

Ella   What do they sell?

Ben   Well, 'Gifts Galore' has little shell animals, polished stones, crystals and all that shit. 'Stars U Like' is all posters and postcards, mainly of Leonardo DiCaprio and the Teletubbies. Then there's 'The Sweet Jar' . . .

Ella   . . . selling pick 'n' mix sweets. Right . . . That's quite a risky line of business, isn't it?

Ben   Not that I've –

Ella (*interrupting*)   I mean, they have to be careful about hygiene, don't they?

Ben   Oh yeah, Bayliss is really keen on enforcing the hygiene regulations. He's got me checking all food-selling premises regularly . . .

Ella   So if you just happened to find a maggot in with the jelly snakes . . .

Ruby   Good night, Hamish.

Ben   Bayliss has got it written into everybody's contracts – one little breach of the hygiene regs –

Ella (*interrupting*)   And he'd get his bailiffs to chuck 'em out?

Ben   You're looking at the bailiff.

Ruby   Put him away.

Ben *flexes his muscles.*

Ben   The problem is, although we can probably get the Sweet Jar folk out, no bother, you're still gonna need to pay Bayliss the rent for their kiosk, at least two months in advance. And those big ones don't come cheap.

Dean   Right in the bottom.

Ella   I'll go see him on Monday.

Ben   I don't reckon you'll knock him down on the price.

Ella   It's always worth a try.

Ben   You can always try your womanly charms, I suppose.

Ella *stretches out.*

Ella   Does Mr Bayliss like womanly charms?

Ben   Nobody knows what he likes.

Ruby   Steady.

Ella   Ah. Is he married . . . or something?

Ben   Used to be . . . She disappeared . . . five or six years ago. Maybe she left him, but there's talk.

Ella   Isn't there always?

Ben   And have you heard about his mum – Old Eliza Bayliss? Died in a boating accident. 'No suspicious circumstances', *they said*. Her ghost's supposed to walk the prom . . .

Ella   No?

Ben   On dark, moonless nights, like tonight, Eliza Bayliss walks wailing the name of her lover.

Ella   Not her husband?

Ben   She had a lover.

Ella   . . . While her old man was knocking off Madame Zara? Right.

Ben   He must've had one weird childhood.

Ella   Edwin?

Ben   Who?

Ruby   You'd have thought he'd be stiffer.

Ruby *exits*.

Ella   Mr Bayliss said I could call him Edwin.

Dean *joins them*.

Ben   How was it for you, our kid?

Dean   What?

Ben   You and Rubes, you grubby little scrote.

Ella   You shagged Ruby? Urh.

Dean   Fuck no! I mean, she's a fucking dog. No offence like . . .

Ella   So what were you doing? Showing her the chocolate flakes?

Dean   No way, man! I don't do that with anybody –

Ella *kicks him*.

Dean   . . . Anybody at all like . . .

Dean *crouches down beside* **Ella**.

Dean   You're not gonna leave tomorrow . . .

Ella   Not tomorrow exactly . . .

Dean   Cos . . . cos I'm gonna take you out. The pictures, dinner and everything, cos you're class, you are . . .

Ben   Dean . . . what did I say to you earlier . . .

QUEEN MARGARET UNIVERSITY LRC

Dean   Look, Ben . . .

Ben   One word, Dean. Starts with an H. Four letters . . .

Dean   A four-letter word starts with H? Er, don't hurry me . . . Er, is it a foreign one?

Ben (*in his face*)   Home. Home, Dean. Gottit? Piss off fucking home, fucking now!

Dean   Yeah, yeah . . . night, Ella babes.

Exit **Dean**.

Ella *gets up*.

Ella   I better be getting back too.

Ben   Ella, wait . . . the night is young.

Ella *looks at her watch*.

Ella   It's five in the fucking morning.

Ben   I'll walk you home . . .

Ella *and* **Ben** *walk up the beach. He puts his arm around her shoulders.*

Ben   Yeah, as I was saying, you've got a . . . a natural flair for business. You'll probably end up seriously successful, like that Body Shop bird.

Ella   I doubt it. Not without a good team behind me.

Ben   You've got me . . . well, and Dean. I know he's an idle little shit but I'm not afraid of a bit of graft. We could be a team, Ella. I mean, behind every tough businesswoman, there's always a tough geezer.

Ella   Drinking her money?

Ben   Sorting out anyone who's giving her grief. Helping her . . . with her wheelings and dealings. You know I can see you being rich, Ella. Incredibly rich, I'm telling you, babe. . . . With the right team behind you, the right kind of support. And now you're going to be staying in town for a while . . .

Ella   I don't know about that. If I'm gonna hang around, I need to find somewhere else to live and fucking quickly. Dad and Turbo Tits'll be back from Ibiza on Monday and when they see the windows they're gonna kill me.

Ben   Turbo Tits?

Ella   It's a long story . . . The problem is, until next week when the money from the dolphin venture starts pouring in . . . I'm a little short of cash . . .

Ben   Look, Ella . . . I could maybe put you up for a bit . . . I've got this place . . . with a few of my mates . . .

Ella   A flat-share? Like *This Life*?

Ben   More of a bungalow/-share.

Ella   /Bungalow, urh.

They reach the kiosk. **Ella** *looks inside.*

Fucking typical, Dean's left the lid off the freezer.

Ben   Useless little scrote.

Ella *goes into the kiosk.*

Ella   If I hadn't noticed, the whole lot would've melted. Tomorrow morning, there'd just be Hamish lying there in a little damp pool.

Ben   Who's Hamish? Lucky bastard.

Ben *leans against the kiosk.*

Ella (*in the kiosk*)   Ooh, we've got Calippos in again.

She pushes up one.

Mmmm.

She sticks the Calippo up above the hatch.

Fancy a lick?

Ben *tries to lick the Calippo.* **Ella** *quickly moves it away.*

Ben   Oy.

Giggling, **Ella** *brings the Calippo back.* **Ben** *snatches it.* **Ella** *lies down on the floor of the kiosk, her bare legs sticking out the door.* **Ben** *licks the Calippo.*

Ella   Great shape, isn't it? What *couldn't* you do with that?

Ben *looks down at her.*

Blackout.

Scene Seven

Ben *is fiddling with a security camera, now positioned at the edge of the café roof. The VCR and monitor are in the café.* **Ella** *is sitting in the café, eating a cake and reading* Cosmo. **Ruby** *is wiping up around her.*

Ella   Another cup of tea would be nice.

Ruby   There ain't no table service.

Ella   You must really like working here.

Ruby *ignores her.* **Ella** *puts her bit of cake down right where* **Ruby** *is trying to wipe.* **Ella** *flicks cake crumbs on the floor.* **Ruby** *glares.*

Ella   Dean says you've been making teas and selling doughnuts for nearly three years. So the job's gotta have something going for it, doesn't it?

Ruby   Mr Bayliss doesn't need any more staff at the moment.

Ella   Oh . . . don't get me wrong, Ruby, I'm not wanting to work here. I mean, no offence, but I couldn't let myself become a skivvy in a place like this.

Ruby   I'm only doing it temporary like.

Ella   Yeah? Three years doesn't seem very temporary to me . . .

Ruby   So? I mean, so what? Since when's what I do become your business?

Ella   It ain't. I'm just trying to put myself in your place . . .

Ruby   You're not having my job! I've been watching you . . . I know your game . . .

Ella   And what game is that, Ruby?

Ruby *goes back behind her counter.*

Ruby   You want a tea you gotta come up here and order it.

Ella *goes to the counter.*

Ella   I'm not after your job. I'm just trying to understand what makes you stay here . . .

Ruby   Mr Bayliss is gonna give me a better job soon. He's talking about improving this place . . .

Ella   Is he now? It looks to me like it's going to rack and ruin.

Ruby   Just a tea was it?

Ella   If it's not putting you to trouble. And how exactly is Mr Bayliss gonna improve things?

Ruby   I . . . I haven't asked him.

Ella   You're up to something though. You must be. You've got some little scheme up your sleeve . . .

Ruby   Scheme? What scheme?

Ella   To make money.

Ruby   I don't do the Lottery, if that's what you're on about. I don't see the point. I mean, what would I do with a couple of million?

Ella Open a cake shop? Ruby . . . if you don't mind me asking . . .

Ruby *shoves the cup of tea to* **Ella**.

Ella Ta. . . . are you shagging Edwin?

Ruby Who?

Enter **Edwin** *into the café.*

Edwin Ella . . . a word.

Ruby Morning, Mr Bayliss.

Edwin Morning, Ruby. A cup of tea would be nice.

Ruby (*smiling*) Coming right up.

Ella *walks past* **Edwin** *to look at the fish.*

Ella The big red-cap looks better now, don't he? . . . must've been my tonic . . . sorted out his swim bladder troubles.

She sits down at a table beside the fish tank, sideways to the table, feet up on a chair. **Edwin** *takes* **Ella**'*s fruit machine book from behind the fish tank. He puts it down on the table in front of her.*

What's that?

Edwin Before you go to great lengths to disassociate yourself from this book, I suggest you take a close look at the front cover. Whoever sent it to you pressed down rather too hard with their biro when addressing the parcel.

Ella *gets up.*

Ella Look, I can explain . . .

Edwin *smiles.*

Edwin Sit down . . . please.

Ella *sits.*

Edwin   Makes fascinating reading, doesn't it? It's funny, I was flicking through it in bed last night, and it reminded me of some of the scams my father used to get up to.

Ella (*relaxing slightly*)   Yeah? Bit of a fruit-machine bandit, was he, your dad?

Edwin   He was a gambler. A good one. Studied form. Treated it as a science. Started with nothing, and built this place up from his winnings.

Pause. **Edwin** *looks at* **Ella**.

Edwin   And he had the same kind of success with women.

Ella   He was skirt chaser too?

Edwin   He didn't have to chase them.

Ruby *brings* **Edwin** *his tea.*

Edwin   Thank you, Ruby.

Ella (*looking at* **Ruby**)   Just rolled over for him, did they?

Ruby *goes back behind the hatch.*

Edwin   Pretty much, yes. At first I couldn't see why . . .

Ella   He was loaded.

Edwin   Not to begin with.

Ella   Was he drop-dead gorgeous or something?

Edwin   No, I wouldn't say he was anything special to look at. Like I said, he studied form, paid attention to detail . . . He'd meet a woman he liked the look of, he'd get some sort of conversation started . . .

Ella   Yeah?

Edwin   He wouldn't say much, but he'd be listening. Really listening. And watching. He'd watch her every slight movement, he'd watch her eyes. Plus he'd notice tiny details . . . He'd see a single hair clinging to her dress, and know whether she had a cat or a dog. Maybe even what breed it was. And he knew how to use that. But the thing was, he never let his emotions get in the way. He just treated it as a game, another jackpot to win.

Ella *sips her tea.*

Ella   And what about you? Do you play too?

Edwin   No.

Ella   Never?

Edwin   But I recognise his techniques when someone's using them on me.

He sips his tea.

And I ask myself why. I'm not so vain as to think you'd be trying to seduce me, Ella . . . So what is it you want?

Ella   Me? I'm sorry I don't know/ what you mean.

Edwin   /I have *The Aquarist* on subscription. I'd read this month's pull-out on fish diseases.

Dean *walks into the café with a lifesize cardboard Liam Gallagher.*

Dean   The bloke said we could have Liam, Noel and Scary Spice all week. But they've got to be back by Saturday morning cos the area manager's coming down. And he wouldn't take a cheque. I said we'd get back to him.

Ella   Cash is fine, if he's prepared to wait until Friday.

Dean   . . . and he's got Darth Vader, Pamela Anderson, Pocahontas and a really big Willy if we're interested.

Ella   Willy?

Edwin *gets up and looks at the cardboard Liam.*

Dean   The whale from *Free Willy 1, 2* and *3*. Kind of look good outside the dolphin kiosk, wouldn't it?

Edwin   I'm sure I've seen him somewhere.

Dean *looks incredulous.*

Ella   Don't get out much, do you, Edwin?

Dean (*loud whisper*)   Ella! He's been *inside*.

Ruby *joins them in time to shoot* **Dean** *a poisonous look.*

Edwin   What I mean, is I've seen this cut-out
somewhere . . .

Dean   In the window of Blockbuster Video.

Ella   We're offering people the once-in-a-lifetime chance
to be photographed with their hero or heroine. For a
reasonable fee of course.

Dean   Who's your hero, Rubes?

Ruby *glances shyly at* **Edwin**.

Ruby   I . . . I don't know really. I . . . I quite like Rolf
Harris.

Ella   What?

Ruby   He's really good with the pets on *Animal Hospital*,
isn't he? Once there was this little hamster with a tumour –
and I cried, it was so moving . . . er, have you finished with
these, Mr Bayliss?

She collects the tea cups.

And he's artistic. Rolf Harris.

Exit **Ruby** *behind the hatch.*

Dean   Get all the others, shall I, then?

Ella   If Edwin doesn't mind us taking up any more space
on the prom.

Edwin   Put them where you like. We can discuss
percentages later.

Exit **Dean**, *leaving the cut-out.*

Ella *sits back down.*

Edwin   Now where were we?

Ella   You were asking me what I'm after . . . when actually I was about to offer you something. A business opportunity.

Edwin (*wearily*)   You want money.

Ella   Everyone wants money. But what I've got is a fail-safe way of making some. The thing is . . . to do it, I need a second kiosk, a bigger one . . . but, cards on the table, I can't afford to pay you the rent up-front this time.

Edwin   My terms are still not negotiable.

Ella   To be honest, Edwin, as one business person to another, I think that's where you're going wrong. It's the start of the season, you've quite a few empty kiosks, but you won't consider reducing the rents or offering more reasonable terms.

Edwin   In my experience if you underprice, you only get time-wasters, and troublemakers.

Ella   Whereas if you overprice, you don't get anyone. Look, Edwin, you can see how well my dolphin venture's doing, and I've not wasted any of your time or been any trouble to you so far, have I? Now what I'm offering is a share of my profits, instead of paying rent. If my sales increase as I've predicted, you'll double your money. If they stay more or less the same, you still won't lose out.

Pause.

Will you at least think about it?

Edwin *gets up, seemingly about to leave. He stops and looks at the fish.*

Edwin   I was up on the pier yesterday afternoon . . . watching the people coming back from seeing the dolphins . . . all getting out of the boat with big smiles on their faces, the children looking like they'd had the time of their life. Years ago, it was easy to make the people forget their troubles on a day at the seaside. Now, though, nothing seems able to break through their cynicism . . . and anger.

People come here just to drink, and fight and smash things. I've spent a small fortune on the security cameras we're currently installing, but you're dealing with the problem another way.

Ella *nods.*

Edwin   It fits in very well with my new vision for this site . . .

Ella   Ruby was telling me about that. It sounds very exciting.

Edwin   It's my intention to make this season the best ever. I want to give people back some of the old magic they found here in the past, to see them smiling and laughing again . . .

Pause. **Edwin** *feeds the fish.*

. . . to make my last summer here something to be remembered by.

Ella   Your last summer – are you selling up?

Edwin   Not exactly . . . Look, I haven't said anything to anyone about this yet . . . but you see . . . I don't have that long to live . . .

Ella   . . . Shit . . .

Edwin   My leg . . . well, it's a tumour/

Ella   /Urh. Are you sure? Someone told me it was something to do with a dog.

Edwin   Not Madame Zara by any chance? She dropped her crystal a while back, and her predictions have been a little lacking in accuracy since then.

Ella   Well, Dean seems to think you've had some kind of accident . . .

Edwin   He probably heard that from Ruby. I told her I'd slipped over. She's . . . a rather sensitive girl . . .

Ella   Yeah, I'd noticed.

Edwin   It seems . . . kinder to let her think that, than to let her know that I'm not long for this earth.

Ella   So you're really gonna die? (*A beat.*) That's serious shit.

Edwin   I suppose it is. But it's made me put things into perspective. Re-evaluate my priorities, if you like . . . which is why I'm thinking of investing in improvements . . . to the pier in particular . . .

Ella   Yeah, the pier's a big let-down. You need to get some *much* scarier rides for a start and more virtual, interactive-type games in the arcades. And as for the 'entertainments' at the Pavilion, I think you should cancel the lot of them for a start.

Edwin   All of them?

Ella   Yeah, the whole shitty lot! Talent shows, crap comedians and bands from the sixties with none of their original members left. Utter wank, innit?

Edwin   I can't see Oasis playing the end of the pier.

Ella   The next Oasis might. Up and coming bands would play here – provided the Pavilion was done up a bit . . . But the old ballroom, that's where you're *really* going wrong. It's completely wasted as a bingo hall. A big venue like that – it has enormous er . . .

Edwin   Potential?

Ella   . . . potential to make big money if we –

Edwin   We?

Ella   Are you just picking my brains or are you offering me something here?

Edwin   What did you used to do?

Ella   When?

Edwin   Jobwise?

Ella   Nothing.

Edwin   Nothing?

Ella   Oh, I don't mean I was sitting on my arse. I was
working for myself . . . You go to the Job Club. They give
you free stamps and you sit there writing job applications.
Actually you write to shops enclosing bits of toenail clipping
you found in their products. You tell 'em you're going to the
papers and environmental health, so the shop phones you,
and offers you gift tokens and stuff. And you know when
you take an item of clothes back to a shop you're supposed
to have the receipt? They can't actually insist on it. It's not
legally binding. So first you go round the shops with a pair
of scissors, and snip out some of the labels. Next, you go
down the market and buy say black or white T-shirts at a
quid a time. You make a little hole in each one, and sew in
the shop labels. Then you return to the high street – where
T-shirts are priced at £12.99 or so each – and ask for your
money back.

Enter **Ruby** *from behind the hatch. She starts wiping a table but is
rather obviously eavesdropping.*

Edwin   So you've business acumen. But can I trust you?

Ella   I could ask you the same question, couldn't I?

Edwin   Right now I've some paperwork I need to finish,
but we must find some time to discuss this matter further . . .
maybe over dinner tonight . . .

Ella   This evening's not good for me, but I can probably
find a window in me diary for tomorrow morning.

Edwin   Very well. Let's have a working breakfast
tomorrow then.

Exit **Edwin**.

Ella *goes outside to* **Ben**.

Ella   Ben. Ben, listen, I've just been talking to Edwin, and
we've as good as got our second kiosk. We've just got to

agree financial terms tomorrow, but it looks like he's gonna let us have it for a bargain price. But that's not all – he's so impressed by the success of my . . . by our dolphin venture, that he's talking about letting us run the old ballroom . . .

Ben   The ballroom? Well, I don't know about you, Ella, but I don't really picture myself as a bingo caller.

Ella   I'm not talking about bloody bingo. I'm talking about turning it into a nightclub. The hottest nightspot on the coast, to be exact. That's where the big money is, Ben. In running a club.

Ben   OK . . . well, it sounds like a . . . a businesslike idea and that . . . but are you sure it's us who're gonna be making those profits, or Mr Bayliss? I mean, if he sees us making serious money, he's sure to find a way to cream most of it off for himself.

Ella   Well, Mr Bayliss won't actually *see* us making anything. We'll be very careful with what we let him find out . . .

Ella *stops, seeing* **Ruby** *in the doorway of the café.* **Ella** *looks at* **Ben**.

Ruby   Will you now?

Ella   Oh, hallo, Ruby. How's things? Still missing your friend Naomi, are you? I have got it right, haven't I? Naomi was your friend, wasn't she?

Ben   Pubes-in-the-coffee Naomi, yeah.

Ella   Dean's been telling me how Mr Bayliss takes matters of hygiene very seriously. So if something like that were to ever happen again . . . Like a punter was to complain about a short and curly in their tea, for example . . .

Ben   . . . Well, there's only one person who could be held responsible, ain't there . . .

Ruby   You can't threaten me. I'm going straight to Mr Bayliss . . .

Ella And just suppose Dean happens to serve a customer with a special new kind of choc ice, from the kiosk's freezer. A small furry choc ice . . .

Ben What's this?

Ella I think we can count on your support for our plans, can't we, Ruby?

Blackout.

Scene Eight

Morning. **Ella** *in the kiosk.*

Ella Slower . . . yeah. Oh, that it's the spot . . . oh, yeah . . . Don't stop!

Edwin *emerges with a flake.*

Ella So that's a business breakfast.

Edwin And now it's about time that I got on with some proper work.

Ella Work's all you think about, innit? God, I mean, with most blokes it's shagging . . .

Edwin I told you I hate that word.

Ella Yeah, yeah . . . I'm just saying that all you think about is business, even though you're fucking dying. I mean, for fuck's sake – why don't you try to chill out and enjoy yourself?

Edwin Old habits, Ella.

Ella Yeah, even while we were shagging – sorry 'making love' your mind was somewhere else, wasn't it? I thought only girls did that – thinking of England. So what were you thinking about anyway? – how to fiddle your tax without getting caught this time?

Edwin I don't know why you have to be so aggressive.

Ella   Aggressive? I thought I was pretty chilled today actually. But you wind me up . . .

Edwin   You need to learn not to let things wind you up.

Ella   I only get wound up cos everything's so fucking unfair. Everywhere I go, it's like screw or get screwed. That's all life's about, innit?

Edwin   Quite possibly, but I don't let it worry me.

Ella   It's no wonder you get on so well with the fucking goldfish. They don't have feelings neither.

Edwin   They do . . . we just can't understand them. Now if you went for a reading with Madame Zara, she'd know everything about you in an instant. It's all too near the surface.

Ella   So people don't know what you're thinking? Big fucking deal. Where does that get you? It pisses people off. I'd probably hit you if you weren't dying and that.

Edwin   You need affection, Ella. And I can't give you that.

Ella   Affection? What good's that? I need money. That's all. And a good laugh, and a good fuck now and again.

Edwin   You're living with Ben, aren't you?

Ella   Not for much longer. One of his housemates said they'd had a couple round looking for me. Gotta be me dad and Turbo Tits.

Edwin   You know where I live?

Ella   Big white house overlooking the crazy golf.

Edwin   You can come and live with me if you like.

Ella   If I like? Is that what you'd like?

Edwin   It would be a convenient arrangement.

Ella   'Convenient', right.

Edwin   Only don't expect affection.

Ella   Fuck affection!

Edwin   I wouldn't charge you rent, of course.

Ella   I should think not. Not if I'm having to shag you and everything. But really . . . I'm very happy at Ben's . . . I guess I'd need a really big . . . er . . .

Edwin   Incentive?

Ella   . . . A really big incentive to move in with you?

Edwin   For example?

Ella   Well, off the top of me head like . . . . what about letting me run the ballroom, like we talked about yesterday.

Edwin   I don't know . . . the thing is, you see, now that I can't get about so well, I was thinking of hiring a site manager to be in charge of developing the larger venues on the site . . .

Ella   So hire me.

Edwin   Do you think you're up to the job, Ella?

Ella   Can you imagine anyone else providing the same level of personal satisfaction? (*Pause.*) Well, maybe you can. Perhaps you've got somebody already lined up for the job. Someone who you'd rather be shagging. Someone like Ruby –

Edwin (*interrupting*)   Ruby! Urgh! Er . . . so I take it you'll accept the position of Site Manager?

Ella   . . . and along with my wages; and accommodation, you'll let me have both my kiosks rent-free for the rest of the summer.

Edwin   No deal. Uh uh.

Ella   One kiosk rent-free?

Edwin   The smaller one.

Ella   You're a stingy git.

Edwin   Do I take it we have a deal?

Ella   I'll need two days off a week.

Edwin   One and a half.

Ella   Double pay for working the extra half.

Edwin   And you're on a two-month probationary period.

Ella   But you can't sack me without good reason. Look, you will put all this . . . contractual shit in writing, won't you?

Edwin   Of course. Now if that's all . . .

Ella   Edwin, call me a nosy bitch if you like . . . but what happened to your wife?

Edwin   She's history.

Ella   Living history or dead history? I mean, I've heard talk . . .

Edwin   There's always talk.

Ella   I suppose what I'm asking is . . . did you murder her?

Edwin *smiles.*

Ella   I mean, if I've shagged a murderer then that's a first for me.

Edwin   I've told you I don't like that word.

Ella   'Murderer'?

Edwin   'Shagged'. And I didn't murder her . . . she ran off . . . with the donkey man . . . nearly six years ago. I've not heard from her since.

Ella   Why was he called the donkey man?

Edwin   Since he didn't work with the donkeys I can only hazard a guess.

Ella   Is my nail varnish down there?

Edwin   Can't see it. There's a bottle of something green . . .

Ella   That's it.

Edwin *holds up the green nail varnish.*

Ella   Nice, innit?

Edwin   No.

Ella   I like you. You're so *old*. Hallo, someone's about.

Edwin *pockets the bottle, without* **Ella** *noticing. He ducks back out of sight.*

Enter **Ruby**.

Ruby   Ella, can I see –

Ella (*interrupting*)   Look, not now, it's right under the new delivery of Cornettos.

Ruby *looks in the hatch, gasps.*

Ruby   Oh . . . morning, Mr Bayliss.

Edwin   Er morning, Ruby. . . . I . . . I was just checking the freezer. In fact it does seem a bit damp in here. Ella, look, some of these boxes are soggy.

Ella   Dean did say he thought it wasn't working properly.

Edwin   Then why on earth didn't he report it?

He opens boxes of ice creams.

Look at these. All soft. And these. And . . .

Ruby *gasps. He has discovered Hamish.*

Edwin   What on earth!!!

Ruby   H . . . H . . . Hamish my hamster.

Edwin   A hamster. In with my ice creams.

Ruby   Can I have him please, Mr Bayliss . . .

Edwin *leaves the kiosk.*

Edwin   Ruby, a word.

Ruby *follows* **Edwin** *to the café.*

Enter **Dean**.

Ella   You're late.

Dean   Since when's it your problem?

Ella   Since I became Site Manager.

Dean   What? Fucking . . .

Edwin *sits* **Ruby** *down at a table, putting Hamish's box on the table in front of her.*

Edwin   Wait there.

Ruby *(upset)*   Yes, Mr Bayliss.

Exit **Edwin**.

Dean   How the fuck did you manage that? Are you shagging the old bugger or something?

Ella *hits* **Dean**.

Ella   Course I'm not fucking shagging him. And now I'm your boss you can start showing me a little respect. And no more slacking, Dean. Now you've got three fully-booked dolphin trips this morning, and the boat needs a wash down before the first lot of punters arrive . . .

Dean   The dolphin trips are a real success, Ella. You must've made loads of dosh on them.

Ella   It's building up steadily . . .

Dean   Steadily? You've been raking it in . . . Must be nearly enough for our plane tickets to Hollywood, eh?

Ella   I reckon we'll have enough by Sunday. When I get a spare minute, I'll ring up about the tickets.

Dean   Sunday! Cool. Uma Thurman, your luck's in, girl!

Ella   But listen, you mustn't say nothing about our leaving to Ben or Mr Bayliss . . . If we have to share the takings with Ben there'll be less for us, and if Bayliss finds out how well the dolphin trips are doing, he'll start wanting a cut and all . . .

Enter **Ben**.

Ella   What time do you call this, Mr Kick-arse Man?

Ben   Think I deserved a bit of a lie-in this morning, don't you – if know what I'm saying?

Ella   I still got up on time.

Ben   It's different for birds – it don't knacker you out . . .

Dean   What doesn't?

Ella   . . . Er, Dean, don't you have a boat to wash down?

Dean   Yeah, yeah.

Exit **Dean**.

Ella   Ben, I've written out a list of jobs for you and –

Ben   Excuse me?

Ella   I've been promoted, Ben.

Ben   To what? From what?

Ella   I'm your new boss.

Ben   Fucking hell! You better be fucking joking.

Ella   Edwin and I had a business breakfast, to talk over our plans.

Ben   I thought they were *our* plans, Ella. I thought you were in business with me.

Ella   I am, Ben. And you'll never guess what? – We've got the ballroom! Now, I think we should start planning our first

club night right away . . . get things up and running for this
Saturday.

Ben   That soon like? That's gonna take a lot of graft.

Ella   That's why I'm in business with you, Ben. Cos you're
a *grafter*. Now your first job of the day is clearing the chairs
and desks out of the ballroom. I'll get on with organising the
lights and music. Any problems I'll be at my desk in Edwin's
office. Well, what're you still standing around for?

Exit **Ben**.

Ella *goes into the ice-cream kiosk, comes out with a flake.*

Enter **Edwin**, *into the café, carrying a booklet.*

Edwin   Do you know what this is, Ruby?

Ruby (*fearfully*)   The Health and Safety guidelines.

Edwin   And you know what has to happen to catering
staff who breach the guidelines?

Ruby   Please, Mr Bayliss. Please don't sack me.

Ella *walks into the café, nibbling the flake.*

Ella   Edwin . . . er, a word.

Edwin   I'm currently dealing with a staff problem, Ella.

Ella   This *is* a staff problem. I need my first month's Site
Managerial wages in advance.

Edwin   We agreed your pay day will be at the end of the
month.

Pause. **Ella** *stands her ground.*

Ella   Then I may well find myself having to take industrial
action . . .

Edwin   On the first day of your probationary period?

Ella   No, on my first night of full duties . . . I may find myself having to severely limit the number of activities I'm willing to perform . . .

She leans over the table. **Ruby** *watches, suspicious.*

Edwin   Alright, just this once . . .

Edwin *takes a chequebook and pen from his pocket, writes out a cheque.*

Edwin   There you are. Anything else?

Ella   I don't think so. Thanks.

Exit **Ella***.*

Edwin *picks up the box containing Hamish.*

Edwin   Now, Ruby, I think we need to get this little matter settled, don't you?

Ruby   Yes, Mr Bayliss. I'm sorry, Mr Bayliss.

Edwin   Now, just imagine if Dean or Ella had gone to serve someone an ice cream, and had instead given them a dead hamster. That would've been rather unfortunate, wouldn't it?

Ruby*'s lip quivers, she's trying not to cry.*

Ruby   Yes, Mr Bayliss.

Edwin   The environmental health officer might've made us close the kiosk. Might've even revoked our licence to sell food, and that would mean the candyfloss, the burger places and *the café* would have had to go too. Now you know I take health and hygiene regulations very seriously . . .

Ruby   It wasn't true about Naomi.

Edwin   We're not talking about Naomi. We're talking about this. (*He indicates Hamish's resting place.*) What I really can't fathom is why you were keeping your . . . departed furry friend's body anyway.

Ruby   I wanted to ask your advice. Only I didn't like to bother you about it while you were . . . *in there*. And since you've been back, I haven't had the chance. You see, I've gotta either find somewhere nice to bury him . . . or would it be alright to cremate him, do you think? I mean, do you think hamsters have a soul? Do they go to heaven?

Edwin *sits back in his chair. He studies the box.*

Edwin   I'm probably not the right person to ask about souls, Ruby.

Ruby   What do you do with your fish, when they . . . pass on?

Edwin   Flush them down the loo. If they're really big ones, like Bronzino there, I chop them up first so they don't stick in the S-bend.

Ruby *looks sick.*

Ruby (*barely controlling her emotions*)   What're you going to do?

Edwin *starts to open the box.*

Ruby   Don't! . . . please.

Edwin *tips the hamster out on the table top. Hamish is very much alive.* **Edwin** *is surprised.* **Ruby** *gasps.*

Ruby   Hamish! (*Pause.*) Oh, Mr Bayliss!

Ruby *hugs* **Edwin**, *awkwardly.*

Edwin   I knew there was something wrong with that freezer . . .

Blackout.

Scene Nine

Ella *is leaning on the 'dolfin' kiosk, going through a checklist with* **Ben**. *In the café,* **Ruby** *has Hamish in a cage on the table. She is feeding him bits of cake.*

Ella   The DJs will be here by seven. Show them where the ballroom is and give 'em the VIP treatment.

Ruby   That's it, stuff your little face.

Ella   Dean's done some more last-minute fly-postering, so there can't be anyone left who's not heard about it. We'll have punters queuing the length of the pier by eight.

She looks down her list.

Security arrangements?

Ruby *eats some cake herself.*

Ben   I've got a strong team together, top blokes. Nobody'll get so much as an aspirin past my doormen . . .

Ella   So everyone'll have to buy from us.

Ruby   A bit for you and a bit for me.

Ella   Edwin wants fifty per cent of door fees and drink profits.

Ben   The old crook!

Ella   But even if we don't cook the books, we'll still clean up on pharmaceuticals . . . which he'll have no idea about. This is gonna make our fortunes, Ben.

Ben   It better. These guys I've got the pills off, they're heavy news. If they don't get their money first thing tomorrow . . .

Ella   They will, trust me, Ben.

Ben   And what about the booze?

Ella *looks at her watch.*

Ella   Should be leaving Dieppe right now. Couple of Stefan's mates are bringing it . . .

Ben   Stefan? Yeah, Dean mentioned this bloke Stefan. I don't know how I've been too thick to realise . . .

Ella   Realise what?

Ben   That he's still your bloke. That it's still going on.

Ben *catches hold of* **Ella**. **Ruby** *goes behind the hatch.*

Ben   Told me you were staying with your mate Leanne . . . and like a mug I believed you, Ella.

Ella *pulls away.*

Ella   Stefan's in London. I've not seen him in months, OK? We're just good friends now. Keep in touch like. Ben, I told you why I had to leave your place. I was frightened for my life . . .

Ben   Your dad and what's-her-name – Big Bazookas –

Ella   Turbo Tits. Dad and Turbo Tits got your address from someone and came looking for me. Honestly, Ben, you've no idea what my dad would do to you if he found out you were hiding me.

Ben   What? I'm not scared of your old man. In my time I've had to sort out quite a few problem dads . . . give 'em a few slaps, it's funny how quick they come round to seeing things from the bird's point of view.

Ella   Yeah, but it's not just him, is it? I mean, it's who he knows, innit?

Ben   Oh yeah, I forgot . . . he's connected. Yeah . . . look, maybe it is better if you've found some . . . safe house to live at or something, if you know what I'm saying. . . . But that doesn't mean we have to stop seeing each other . . .

Ella   No of course it doesn't . . . though I dunno how much time I'm gonna have to . . . socialise with my staff from now on . . .

Ben   Your staff, bollocks! We have a relationship, girl.

Ella's *mobile rings.* **Ella** *takes it out.*

Ella   Edwin gave me this. Cool, eh? (*On phone.*) Yeah,
speaking. What? Fuck . . . did it? Right. (*To* **Ben**.) Fuck
Edwin. Fucking cheque bounced. Fucking bastard. How am
I gonna pay for the booze now?

Enter **Dean** *running, breathless and wet.*

Dean   Calamity, man! – the dolphins have gone ballistic!

Ella   What?

Dean   I've a boat full of punters right? We're just out
beyond the end of the pier and the dolphins are going
through their paces. Then they stop, and turn so they're
facing the boat, and suddenly they start swimming straight
towards us. The punters are all getting excited, getting their
cameras and binoculars out. I'm starting to worry, cos if the
dolphins get any closer, the punters are gonna start hearing
the motors –

Ben   Motors?

Dean   I went to grab the remote control/ to send them
away, and the joystick comes off in my hand!

Ben   /Remote control?

Dean   /The dolphins are coming straight for us, all the
punters are standing up to get a better view. I tell 'em to sit
down – they're rocking the boat. They won't listen. They all
rush to the same side of the boat. We tip over, as the
dolphins go bombing past. It's lucky we nicked those
lifejackets from the yacht club, but the punters are
demanding a refund and compensation.

Ella   Never mind them, how are we gonna get our
dolphins?

Ben   They'll come back, if this is their home like. Maybe they were a bit frightened by all the people waving their cameras and –

Ella   My God, didn't I ever tell you? They're not real dolphins, Ben. I had meant to tell you, honest. They're lifesize inflatables mounted on motorised model boats.

Ben   What? (*Pause.*) . . . You . . . you mean it's not Poppy and Smartie from the dolphinarium?

Dean   You were fooled, Ben. He dived in to swim with them. He was calling out 'Poppy, Smartie, here, girls'.

Ben *takes a swipe at* **Dean**. **Ella** *goes to the dolphin hut, takes some out money and a cardboard box full of packing material.*

Ella   Dean, go give 'em their money back, free tickets if they come back tomorrow, and a snow-scene for each of the kids . . . this batch are leaky anyway. (*Pause.*) So where are the dolphins now?

Dean   When I lost sight of 'em they were heading in that direction – er nautical left.

Ella   Dean – quick, go give the whingers their refunds, then get back out there and find those dolphins!

Exit **Dean**, *with the money and box of dolphin snow-scenes.* **Ella** *and* **Ben** *walk towards the café.*

Ben   Why didn't you tell me?

Ella   Like I said, it slipped my mind.

Ben   So where *are* the real Poppy and Smartie? I remember reading in the paper that they were being released into the wild.

Ella   But not in the English Channel.

Ben   We just better hope Dean gets to those bogus dolphins before any of the public or the papers get to hear of it. The last thing we need now is all the punters wanting their money back.

Ben *goes to the security camera on the edge of the café roof.* **Ella** *follows.*

Ben   Got this camera facing the pier . . . maybe there'll be something on the film . . . like if they've floated inshore . . . or if there's some kind of funny business going on . . . You know . . . *Sabotage* . . . Well, it's a thought, innit?

Ella   We're gonna be up shit creek if they don't turn up.

Ben   You're gonna be, you mean? You owe me to the tune of a couple of grand, easy . . . rent for the boat, the first kiosk, money for the stock, not to mention that crap ring. Now I've got the drug dealers' money to worry about, me rent's in arrears, and both me credit cards are heading for fucking meltdown. I've invested a lot of dosh and put my trust in you. For fuck's sake don't let me down, Ella, or it'll all end in tears . . . know what I'm saying?

Ella   Relax . . . once Edwin pays me a cheque I *can* cash –

Ben   Do you really think he will?

Ella   I'm not lifting another fucking finger for him until he bloody coughs it up.

Ben   Look, Ella, I know Bayliss is almost my uncle and everything . . . but he's still a weasely little geezer. I'm saying I think you've made a bad move by getting involved with him . . . I wouldn't trust him as far as I could throw him.

Ella   Who said anything about trusting him? But we need some of what he's got. We need those opportunities. When we're running club nights in the old ballroom *every* Saturday and got top bands playing the Pavilion, it'll be you and me taking the money, you and me making a killing. There's no way Edwin's gonna find out how much we're creaming off. I've got it all planned out, don't you worry. We're a team, remember? We're entrepreneurs . . . And by the end of the season we'll be on our way to being millionaires!

She kisses him. He responds enthusiastically. She pulls away. **Ben**
*looks at the monitor in the café, then goes and adjusts the security
camera. He returns to the binoculars.*

Ben   Fuck me!

Ella   I told you, Ben, I don't have the time –

Ben   Look through the fucking binoculars, quick!

Ella *joins him and looks through them.*

Ella   Is it the dolphins? What am I looking for?

Ben   The end of pier.

Ella   Madame Zara? Is that her motorbike and sidecar?

Ben   Looks like she's packing her bags . . . now that *is*
strange, she'd told me she wasn't leaving 'til the end of the
summer.

Ella   Never mind fucking Madame Zara, where're my
bleedin' dolphins? Alert the coastguard. Just say we've lost a
couple of 'promotional inflatables'.

Exit **Ben**.

Ella *takes down the sign from the dolphin kiosk, starts chalking on the
other side 'Cancelled Due To Circumstances Beyond Our Control'.*

Enter **Edwin** *into the café.* **Ella** *spots him and follows him in.*

Edwin   Ella – cup of tea?

Ella   I just got a call from my bank and guess what?

Edwin   Cheque bounced? I meant to mention it last night,
at supper, but what with one thing an another . . .

Ruby *comes out from behind the hatch.*

Ruby   Afternoon, Mr Bayliss.

Ella   You must have some money you can pay me from.

Edwin   Yes of course, I just wasn't thinking . . . wrote you a cheque on the wrong account . . . the one the Revenue emptied . . . but I've brought my other chequebook with me so I can give you your wages . . .

Ella   You couldn't pay me cash instead? I mean, I owe one or two people round here . . .

Edwin   Well, unfortunately I don't carry much about with me as a rule . . . and it's not very easy for me to go into town at the moment . . . so if you could bear with me . . .

He stretches his bad leg to make the point. **Ruby** *joins them.*

Ruby (*brightly*)   Did you say you need something in town?

Edwin *gives* **Ruby** *a look.*

Ella   That's a thought, innit? . . . Ruby could go to the bank for you . . .

Ruby   Yeah, no problem. I need to go to the pet shop, get some proper food for Hamish.

Edwin   Alright . . . (*To* **Ruby**.) I'll give you my card and pin.

Enter **Ben**.

Ben   Afternoon, Mr Bayliss. Ella, have you got a minute?

Ella *joins* **Ben** *outside.* **Edwin** *gives* **Ruby** *his bank card.*

Ruby   See ya later, Hamish.

Exit **Ruby**.

Ella   Well?

Ben   Nothing on the tape . . . . but fucking Greenpeace are coming! Had me short-wave set on. Apparently a fisherman's spotted 'an injured dolphin' near the entrance to the harbour.

Ella   Shit, we better get down there quick . . .

Ben   . . . Before the bleedin' hippies show up, yeah.

Exit **Ella** *and* **Ben**.

Edwin *looks at his watch. He takes something from his pocket. It is* **Ella**'s *green nail varnish. He opens it, stirs the contents, puts it back in his pocket. He takes out a cigarette lighter and tests it. He looks around, then gets up, without his crutches, walks quickly behind the hatch. He emerges, with two cans of paraffin in Waitrose carrier bags and leaves the café, checking no one is about. He uses his crutch to knock the security camera so it is pointing in the opposite direction. He sloshes paraffin on the ice-cream and dolphin kiosks, then exits making a trail of paraffin behind him.*

Blackout.

Enter **Ella**.

She looks through the binoculars on the prom, then goes to adjust the security camera. Seeing it is pointing the wrong way she adjusts it to face the pier once more.

Exit **Ella**.

A small explosion, suddenly there is fire and smoke everywhere. Light from the fire illuminates the kiosks, and smokes pours from them. The café, though, remains in darkness.

Gradually the fire dies.

Return to blackout.

Scene Ten

Dawn. Smoke billows from the blackened dolphin kiosk and ice-cream hut. **Edwin** *sits in the slightly charred café.* **Ben** *and* **Dean** *sit on the beach, huddled in their parkas, between two huge, smiling dolphin inflatables.*

Ruby *comes out from behind the café hatch with a tray with a cup of tea and selection of fondant fancy cakes. She takes it to* **Edwin**.

Edwin   Who'd have thought it, eh?

Ben *skins up.*

Dean   It could've been an accident, right? Sometimes . . . she used to start fires accidentally. I mean, when she has sex . . . it causes spontaneous combustion, y'know?

Ben   It causes what?

Dean   When she has sex, things catch light.

Ben   Bollocks.

Dean   How do you –

Ben   Cos I've shagged her . . .

Dean *attacks* **Ben**. **Ben** *throws him off.*

Ben   Behave.

Dean   Ella says you never!

Ben   Yeah, Ella says.

Dean *attacks* **Ben** *again.*

Dean   Ella'd never shag you. She's a top bird.

Ben   Believe that if it makes you happy.

Ruby   I never trusted her.

Ben   Anyway Bayliss says the police have got some evidence. Something the Old Bill found where the fire started. And if it's got nothing to do with Ella, then how come they took her away in a panda?

Ruby   Why'd she do it?

Edwin   I don't know her very well, but she strikes me as being a rather unhappy girl.

Ruby   She's hard.

Dean *walks away from* **Ben**, *kicks some pebbles.*

Enter **Ella**, *wearing her jacket and carrying a suitcase. She looks like she hasn't slept.*

Dean   Ella!

Ben *and* **Dean** *join her.* **Ruby** *starts attacking a cake with a knife.*

Ella   Half the fucking night in a police cell. They thought I did it – can you believe that?

Ruby   Bitch.

Dean   Er, they questioned us too, didn't they, Ben?

Ruby   Bitch.

Ella   Didn't drag you down the nick though, did they?

Ben   Didn't find any reason to suspect *us*, did they, Dean?

Ruby   Bitch.

Ella   Yeah, just my luck the fucking fire brigade found bits of a green nail varnish bottle on a ledge below the pier deck. And for some reason they thought it had something to do with me.

Ben (*looking at* **Dean**)   Er, right . . .

Ruby   Bitch.

Ella   They reckon somebody must've climbed down there, set light to it, and legged it before the whole fucking deck went up.

Ruby   Bitch.

Dean   Well, we've got an alibi, Ben and me – we were still fishing the bloody dolphins out the harbour.

Dean   It'll be alright, El. The pigs've let you go, so they can't seriously think you did it . . .

Ruby   They should lock her up and throw away the key!

Ella   I'm supposed to go back later. They must be fucking joking. Soon as it gets light, I'm getting the first train up to London. I've been trying to ring Stefan to get him to meet me.

Ruby   Least you've still got your goldfish, Mr Bayliss.

Ella *looks at her watch.*

Ben   You can't leave . . . not while you owe me.

Dean   Have you got my plane ticket with you?

Ben   What plane ticket?

Dean   Me and Ella are going to Hollywood, today.

Ben   What?!

Dean   She's already got the plane tickets, haven't you, Ella?

Ella   Dean, listen –

Dean   Haven't you! Ella!

Ben *shoves* **Dean**, *sends him sprawling.*

Ben   Is this true? Is it? Were you and . . . him reckoning on leaving the country? After last night's club night?

Ella   No!

Dean   Yes!

Ben   No doubt with all the takings.

Ella   Ben, listen, I don't have any plane tickets. I don't know what he's on about. Well, I do, but it's all a big mistake.

Ben   Yeah, *your* big mistake.

Ella   I'd said to Dean I'd take a holiday with him . . . a couple of weeks in the Hollywood sunshine, paid for with *my* share of last night's profits . . .

Ben   Yeah? Only now there ain't gonna be any profits, are there? And I've got three seriously pissed-off drug dealers breathing down my neck.

Dean   At least the pier went up before tonight's punters started arriving. And Mr Bayliss managed to get all the tourists evacuated.

Ben   I knew the fire drill would work – he's always making us practise it.

Ella   How's Edwin taking it?

Dean   Bad.

Ben   Worse than bad.

Ella   I better go and see him . . .

Ben *stops her going towards the café.*

Ben   Dunno if that's such a good idea like.

Dean   Not 'til you've like totally cleared your name.

Ella   What?

Ben   I think he suspects you of starting the fire.

Dean   That's what he said to us.

Ella   Course I didn't. And I'm going in there to tell him so – and get him to pay me what he owes me – by cash this time.

Ben   Look, maybe we better come with you, just to be on the safe side . . .

Ella *walks towards the café.* **Ben** *and* **Dean** *walk with her carrying the inflatable dolphins.*

Ben   We'll wait out here. If he starts getting heavy just whistle.

Dean   You do know how to whistle, don't you?

Ella *enters the café.*

Ella   Alright, Edwin, Rubes.

Edwin *looks slightly surprised to see her.* **Ella** *sits down, helps herself to a cake.*

Ella   I was so, so sorry to hear about what happened.

Edwin   Er, Ruby, could you make us a fresh pot of tea?

Exit **Ruby.**

Are you OK?

Ella   Never felt better.

Edwin   The police let you go, finally? I was going to ring them . . . tell them it must all be a mistake.

Ella (*sarky*)   You were *going* to ring them? Yeah, right. I was shouting for you to help me when they were like reading me my fucking rights . . .

Edwin   I'm sorry . . . I didn't hear you . . . in all the noise and smoke, with firemen rushing around everywhere . . .

Ella   I was sitting in my cell thinking, Edwin must realise soon there's like a massive miscarriage of justice happening here. I waited and waited.

Edwin   I wasn't aware they'd arrested you.

He stretches his bad leg painfully.

I suppose I was in a kind of shock . . .

Ella (*more sympathetically*)   Yeah . . . OK, that's understandable. You've lost everything, haven't you?

Edwin   Pretty much.

Ella   At least the place was comprehensively insured, wasn't it? I mean, that probably doesn't seem much of a consolation right now, but in a few weeks you'll probably be thanking your lucky stars that you had such a good policy.

Edwin   You seem to know a lot about it.

Ella   Yeah, well, my dad flogs insurance, don't he?

Edwin   I'd got the impression . . . that your father was some kind of gangland figure . . .

Ella   Gangland? (*She laughs.*) I bloody wish. Funny thing is, he used to hope I'd follow in his footsteps. You know, when I was a kid he used to take me door to door with him. People were more likely to let him in if he'd got a kid with him. He'd get me to ask to use the loo, or say I was thirsty.

Then instead of just collecting their premium, he'd have a chance to sit them down and sell them an additional policy. He was regional salesman of the year three years running . . . mainly due to me.

Edwin   This is where you get your . . . business acumen from, is it?

Ella *chokes on her fondant fancy.*

Ella   I don't take after him! He's a tosser, a bullshit merchant, he doesn't know the meaning of sincerity. You know, he taught me to breathe all kind of wheezy . . . then he'd tell people we visited I had bad asthma . . . and persuade them how important it was to insure your children against illness. Once I shouted out 'He's lying, it's all lies!' Must've been about ten, I suppose. After that I stopped going to work with him . . . but like you with your dad, I've learnt to recognise his tricks when other people are using them . . . you know, like faking illnesses and stuff.

Edwin *looks slightly worried.*

Ella   . . . And there were the tales he'd hear from the loss adjusters . . . how after something like a fire, their suspicions would be triggered by little things . . . like certain personal possessions escaping unharmed . . .

She looks at the fish, then back at **Edwin***.*

. . . something happening to lure staff away . . . something a bit like our dolphins disappearing for example . . . and other people changing their routines on the day of the blaze . . . When Ben and me saw Madame Zara leaving, it got me thinking . . .

Edwin   The police and fire brigade don't seem to share your suspicions. Of course, it's early days but I heard arson being mentioned. I believe they've isolated the place where it started . . . beneath the pier deck . . . only reachable by a *precarious* rusting iron ladder . . .

He gets up slowly on his crutches.

Which of course puts me out of the picture.

Ella   Naturally. Can I have another cake?

Edwin   Help yourself.

Ella *takes another cake.*

Ella   Edwin . . . when you were inside . . . what was the food like?

Edwin   That's a very strange question . . .

Ella   Only my boyfriend used to be a chef at Ford. That's where you were, wasn't it?

Edwin   . . . I remember a chef that got sacked . . . for wearing pink stilettos in the kitchen.

Ella   That was Stefan. And he remembers you too. Remembers you when you still had two good legs. Must've been, what, less than a month ago. I suppose these tumour things come on quick when they come.

Edwin   I know what you're trying to do. But I don't think the police are particularly interested in the condition of my leg . . . particularly since I believe they have an item of incriminating evidence.

Ella   Yeah, they told me that much. And they wanted to take photos of my feet. Can't think why.

Pause.

Edwin   Look, how the fire started and why it started is neither here nor there. I need to put all that behind me now, and think to the future. I've some ambitious plans for this site. And if you stop troubling yourself . . . about things like insurance details and medical matters, there might still be a place here for you.

Enter **Ruby** *with the tea.*

Edwin   You could consider a new career as manager of my new Marine World Centre. I'll be applying to demolish the few remaining structures on the pier deck, and to build in their place the largest and best-stocked aquarium in Europe.

Ruby   I'm gonna be feeding all the fish.

Ella   Yeah, well, it's a shame I'm having to leave the country, innit?

Edwin   Do you think the police will allow that, Ella?

Ella   Yeah. Once they see the video.

Edwin   Video?

Ella   From the security camera facing the pier . . .

Edwin *looks round and sees that the camera is indeed now facing the pier. He jumps up, without his crutches.* **Ella** *hands them to him.* **Ruby** *looks on, amazed.*

Edwin   Ruby, go and see if there're any of those delicious fondant fancies left.

Exit **Ruby**.

Edwin *goes to check the VCR, finds there is no tape.*

Edwin   Where is it?

Ella   Sit down, please.

Edwin *moves towards* **Ella**. *She jumps up and backs up.*

Ella   Dean and Ben are outside. If you come near me . . . they'll fucking have you!

Edwin   Ella, you're always so needlessly aggressive . . .

Sound of a police siren, distant. **Edwin** *starts.*

Do the police have the video?

Ella   No. (*Pause.*) I hid it, OK?

Edwin   You hid it? I see. And what, should I wish obtain it, must I do to?

Ella Pay me ten grand. Cash.

Edwin As soon as the insurance business is settled . . .

Ella Ten grand now.

Edwin I don't have it. You'll just have to wait. To be patient, Ella.

Ella Fuck you! Why'd you fucking do it! Why fuck me over? I could've really made something of this place . . . tonight's club night alone would've brought in thousands . . .

Edwin So that you and your stiletto-wearing chef could've been on the next plane to LA, with my money? You see, I've continued to do my homework on you as well.

Ella Is it all a game to you? Fucking me over before I could do it to you. All about winning the fucking jackpot!

Edwin You need to learn how to be a good loser, Ella.

Ella Loser – excuse me. I don't see you sipping the champagne in the winners' enclosure without that video tape.

Edwin So it looks like we're going to have to do a deal here.

Ella What can you offer me?

Edwin *takes out his wallet.*

Edwin I've maybe twenty pounds in cash.

Ella Fuck off.

Edwin My house, my car . . . everything's tied up with this place, I won't be able to lay my hands on more than this for weeks.

Ella Give me that then.

Edwin Give me the tape.

Ella For twenty poxy quid.

Edwin   Take what's on offer and be glad you didn't walk away a loser. Some games have no jackpot, Ella.

Pause. **Ella** *moves to take the money.*

Edwin   The tape first. Then it's yours.

Pause.

Ella   I don't have the fucking tape. I lied. Why do you think the pigs let me go so easily? I had to give it them. Didn't have no choice.

Edwin *turns away.*

Ella   I had to.

She walks towards him.

I'm sorry. And I just want you to know . . . I'd never had grassed on you, if you hadn't of set me up.

Edwin *turns back towards her.*

Edwin   You're sorry. Crying out for affection again. You'll never make it in business, Ella, if you believe in nonsense like honour among thieves.

Ella   I was gonna use the tape to blackmail you.

Edwin *discards the crutches, and grabs* **Ella**. **Dean** *and* **Ben** *rush in.* **Edwin** *and* **Ella** *kiss each other desperately.* **Dean** *and* **Ben** *stop in their tracks, look at one another.*

Ben   Fucking hell!

Enter **Ruby** *with the tray of fondant fancies. She drops it, and exits.*

Dean   Shit.

Ella *almost manages to lift* **Edwin**'s *wallet, but he realises in time to stop her. They stand looking at each other.*

Ella   . . . I'll . . . I'll see you around . . .

Sound of police sirens.

. . . maybe.

She goes outside, followed in silence by **Dean** *and* **Ben**. *She stops at her suitcase.*

You guys've gotta see this.

Edwin   Ruby.

Ella *takes a book, still partly wrapped in brown paper from her case.*

Ella   Sneaked into my house before dad and Turbo Tits woke up this morning. Needed the rest of me clothes see? And I found this parcel waiting for me.

Edwin (*calls*)   Ruby.

Ella *unwraps the book. It is called* How To Succeed As A Confidence Trickster. *She offers it to* **Ben**. *He doesn't take it.* **Ella** *flicks through the book.*

Enter **Ruby**.

Edwin   Call me a taxi, please.

Ruby   Call it your . . . *f* . . . *fucking* self, Mr Bayliss.

Edwin *looks at her for a moment and exits, running, as blue police lights flash along the prom.*

Ben   You were shagging him, weren't yer?

Ruby *picks up a fallen chocolate fondant fancy and crams it in her mouth.*

Ben   Spent all my fucking money and you were shagging him.

Ella   What? You gotta be joking.

Dean (*sarky*)   Yeah, right.

Ben   I wasn't born yesterday . . .

Ella   Ben, listen –

Ben   I've listened all I'm gonna listen. You owe me a lot of money, girl . . . and I'm gonna get it . . .

Ella   Course you are . . . look at this . . .

She holds the book up in front of **Ben**.

Page ten – a card scam you can pull on the train. I reckon
we can make a hundred quid easy by the time we get to
Victoria . . . that's half of one of our plane tickets. Dean, did
you tell Ben about all the business opportunities in LA?

Ben *throws the book down.*

Ben Ella . . . if you weren't a bird . . . and I didn't have a
policy of never doing violence to a bird . . . Look, I've gotta
be getting off home. Been a long night, if you know what
I'm saying, and I ain't had no breakfast . . .

Dean Same 'ere.

Ella There'll be a buffet car on the train. Guys, I've just
about enough to treat you both to a hot toastie . . .
providing you don't want anything too fancy as a filling.

Ben Ella, let me spell this out . . . you've fucked up big
time –

Ella (*interrupting*) It's a temporary set-back, that's all it is . . .

Ben Bullshit.

Ben *starts to move away.*

Ella So you think you'll better off without me, is that what
you're saying?

Ben In a word, yeah.

Ella Wake up, look around you, Ben. Bayliss won't need a
kick-arse man where he's going . . .

Ben I'll find something else.

Ella I'm offering you something else. A first-class
opportunity . . .

Ben . . . to lose the roof over me head, and the clothes off
me back.

Ben *starts walking away.*

Ella   Ben . . . Ben, this is different . . .

She hesitates, about to run after him, but suddenly sees **Dean** *has picked up and is reading the book.*

He'll never get anywhere in life, your brother.

Dean   Look, Ella . . .

Ella *indicates the book.*

Ella   What do you think, eh? Is that a good scam or what?

Dean   You told me you weren't shagging Ben . . .

Ella   Ben? – oh, it's over with Ben now, innit?

Dean   And then I see you and Bayliss . . . You and fucking Bayliss, for fuck's sake.

Ella   Me and Ben, Me and Bayliss? What's your problem? That's all finished, that's my past. I'm thinking of the future here. You and me teaming up, you and me on the make. Don't you want to be rich, Dean? Don't you want to be rich and living in Hollywood?

Dean   And Stefan – the perv? Where's he fit in then? He's still your bloke, ain't he?

Ella *shrugs.*

Ella   Until he's got that job with his uncle, and got me and you in with the all stars. Then we can do as we like. The sky's the limit.

Dean   Yeah, well, I'm just saying I've got me own plans.

Dean *hands her the book back. He goes and sits down on the beach.* **Ella** *stops, impatient.*

Ella   OK. Fine.

Dean   I think I might stop here . . .

Ella   Up to you, innit? If you like living with your parents, having no money, selling fucking ice creams in the summer, just dossing about in the winter . . . I mean, what else you gonna do round here?

Dean   . . . I might take a course . . .

Ella (*sarky*)   Bollocks.

Dean   Or I might just have some other plans, y'know . . .

Ella *shrugs.*

Ella   Alright. OK. Suit yourself, Dean.

She picks up her case and begins to walks off.

Ruby *is pigging out on cakes big time.*

Ella (*without looking back*)   What more can I say? If you're not interested in earning a new pair of Nikes by the end of the day . . . complete designer wardrobe by the end of the week . . . all the beers you can drink, and all the dope you can smoke . . . If you don't want to meet Uma Thurman . . . then OK, you stay here, as King of the Slackers, that's fine by me . . .

She stops, looks back.

. . . I don't need you. I don't need anyone.

Dean *doesn't move.*

Ella   I don't give a shit.

Exit **Ella**.

Dean *gets up. He goes into the ice-cream kiosk, takes a Cadbury's Flake from a box, leans out the hatch, eating it.* **Ruby** *stops eating cakes, goes back behind the hatch and starts writing a sign.* **Dean** *comes into the café.* **Ruby** *puts up the sign. It says 'Business as usual'.*

Dean   Ruby.

Ruby   What?

Dean   Don't still have Naomi's phone number, do you?

Blackout.